Leisure, and the Good Life

Few civilizations have agreed with America that unremitting labor and ceaseless productive enterprise constitute what used to be called "the good life." Not even Victorian England, where, faithful readers of Dickens will remember, when a man acquired some wealth "in the City," he retired as fast as possible to the country to raise huge families of young ladies and gentlemen who would never have to work at all. No, the good life in most times and places has been a life of leisure, or rather a mode of life made possible by large allotments of free time.

Beginning on page 4 of this issue there appears a gleaming array of leisured modes of life that different civilizations have practiced and polished in the past. In ancient Athens, for example, leisure meant a citizen's life of talk and politics in the public places of the city; in imperial China it meant a life devoted to exquisite hobbies.

Alas, the leisured life in contemporary America is somewhat confusing and unsatisfying. Witness the report on affluent Marin County, California, beginning on page 26. America, caught between its old devotion to work and its unparalleled wealth, no longer enjoys a widely accepted conception of what the good life is.

To spend a lifetime in toil made profound

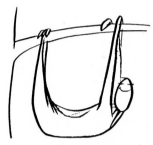

"Leisure" by Robert Osborn

sense when we were laying the foundation of a great productive economy. Now that we are reaping the abundant fruits, work has inevitably lost its former legitimacy. What, we may well ask, is our abundance for? Without an answer to that question that men can agree on and respect, every mode of life adopted by individual Americans will have its portion of anxiety and discontent: is this the way a man should live? What is more, we begin to accept all too easily various unworthy substitutes for that undefined good life, as when we habitually refer to "the standard of living" when we really mean the standard of consumption—a very different matter.

Does the widespread unrest manifest last year in so many different ways, in so many different places, have anything to do with the question of

AMERICAN HERITAGE PUBLISHING CO.	EDITOR
	Joseph J. Thorndike

PRESIDENT
James Parton

MANAGING EDITOR: Charles L. Mee, Jr.
ARTICLES EDITOR: Robert Cowley   ART EDITOR: Jane Wilson
ART DIRECTOR: Kenneth Munowitz

EDITORIAL COMMITTEE
Joseph J. Thorndike, *Chairman*
Oliver Jensen
Richard M. Ketchum

ASSOCIATE EDITORS: Shirley Tomkievicz, Barbara Klaw, Nancy Kelly
CONTRIBUTING EDITOR: Walter Karp
ASSISTANT EDITORS: Priscilla Flood, Mary Sherman Parsons
COPY EDITOR: Mary Ann Pfeiffer   *Assistant:* Carol R. Angell

SENIOR ART DIRECTOR
Irwin Glusker

SENIOR EDITOR, HORIZON
Marshall B. Davidson

ADVISORY BOARD: Gilbert Highet, *Chairman*, Frederick Burkhardt, William Harlan Hale, John Walker

PUBLISHER, HORIZON
Paul Gottlieb

EUROPEAN CONSULTING EDITOR: J. H. Plumb, *Christ's College, Cambridge*
EUROPEAN BUREAU: Gertrudis Feliu, *Chief, 11 rue du Bouloi, Paris 1er*

Horizon

A Magazine of the Arts

SPRING, 1969 · VOLUME XI, NUMBER 2

the good life? The answer, very probably, is yes. At bottom, what the rebels of 1968 had in common was a deep discontent with what they sometimes called the "consumer society." They voiced, as noisily as they could, the kind of puzzled dissatisfaction that their parents' generation only feels intermittently. We are going through a kind of historic upheaval in which the old ways of life developed in harsher times no longer answer to our new condition of prosperity.

If we think, however, that the unrest of 1968 was lawless and violent, it may be instructive to turn to page 66 of this issue. There begins a vivid account of the wild epidemic of riots and insurrections that swept across Europe in that *annus mirabilis*, 1848. Then as now, industrialism was a prime mover of events, but the contrast between 1968 and 1848 is revealing. Then, the upheaval was caused in great measure by the sudden explosion of raw, modern industrialism. Today it has its roots in the bland abundance that advanced industrialism has produced. Then, thoughtful men worried about how the mass of workers could survive under the burden of the new factory system. Today we must worry about how we can live well. Despite the many ironies of history, this looks suspiciously like Progress.   W.K.

HORIZON is published every three months by American Heritage Publishing Co., Inc. Editorial and executive offices: 551 Fifth Avenue, New York, N.Y. 10017. Treasurer: George W. Breitkreuz. Secretary: John C. Taylor 3rd. All correspondence about subscriptions should be addressed to: HORIZON Subscription Office, 379 West Center St., Marion, Ohio 43302.

Single Copies: $5.00; Subscriptions: $16.00 per year in the U.S. & Canada; elsewhere, $17.00

A cumulative index for Volumes I–V is available at $3; a cumulative index for Volumes VI–X will be available this spring. HORIZON is also indexed in the *Readers Guide to Periodical Literature*. The editors welcome contributions but can assume no responsibility for unsolicited material. Title registered U.S. Patent Office. Second class postage paid at New York, N.Y., and at additional mailing offices.

COVER: Two wild cows, long-extinct creatures of the Ice Age woodlands of southern France, appear on a ceiling of the famous Lascaux cave. They are among the hundreds of animals drawn on those underground walls some fifteen thousand years ago. Who did the remarkable murals? For what purpose? And more puzzling yet, for whom were they done? In an article that begins on page 94 Roy McMullen grapples with these and other enigmas of this early art masterwork. The photograph was taken by Romain Robert—Cultural History Research, Inc.

Leisure

It may be a new problem for the masses, but the classes have

A few years ago, as more and more deep thinkers pondered the consequences of automation and the affluent society, it became fashionable to worry about how mankind was going to adjust to a world where the necessary work would be performed in a few brief hours a week, leaving vast cavities of time to be nervously filled, lest we fall into a monstrous indolence that would make the lotus-eaters look like coal miners. This magazine, for example, published a searching article by Dennis Gabor called "The Perils of Leisure" (November, 1963); *Life* came along soon after with a rather solemn study, "Too Much Leisure."

Well, the years have gone by pretty fast, and if too much leisure is a problem, it is not one that seems yet to afflict most of us. You hear few complaints, from anyone over fifteen, about having "nothing to do." Undoubtedly, statistics could show that the average American is gradually spending fewer hours a week at his regular job; but so far, for that same average American, television, spectator sports, and do-it-yourself projects seem to have had no trouble filling the time when he is not assiduously moonlighting.

No, if leisure really is to become a problem, it seems likely that it will be in terms of quality, not quantity. We have not thought enough about *how* we want to spend our free time, how-

ever extensive it may be. Perhaps, indeed, we have not thought enough about what leisure really means, or ought to mean.

The experience of the past is valuable here; we are insulting history if we assume that earlier civilizations have not considered the problem and found solutions that seemed suitable to their views of life. What did the Greeks and Romans think, and what did they do, about extensive leisure? Or the Chinese of old; or the Persians —did they really settle the whole thing underneath a tree, with a book of verses, a loaf of bread, a jug of wine, and a girl with a nice voice box? The editors of HORIZON intend, in this issue, to offer answers to these as well as to some other interesting questions about leisure.

As a preface, it is well to remember that leisure in American civilization has always been a bit suspect, especially among those who have had little of it. The Bible set a ratio of six to one for work versus rest, and even at that the New England idea of the Sabbath was fraught with a sense of pious self-denial: abstention from carnal joys, prayer and meditation, uncomfortable clothes. Leisure, the way the British pronounce it, rhymes with pleasure, and everyone with a Puritan ancestor has a lingering doubt as to how much of that will still let you stay clear of Hell. If you're of an etymological turn of mind, you may also have noted that leisure comes from the same Latin root (*licere*) as license,

which on the respectable side means permission of the authorities and on the other side conjures up visions of orgies. "License they mean when they cry libertie," John Milton said, sounding like a seventeenth-century J. Edgar Hoover: he was against license. Nevertheless, he managed to give a description of Adam and Eve's life after their daily gardening chores were done that has made Paradise a metaphor for sensually gracious leisure ever since.

After your tasks are done—that may be the key to the true meaning of leisure. It goes beyond the simple concept of leisure as whatever time is left over at the end of the regular working day. We all have promises to keep, and it is only with the feeling that our obligations—our *devoirs*, as the French nicely put it—are at least temporarily discharged that we can experience the true sense of leisure. It is a highly subjective thing, connected with what old-fashioned people call conscience, and individuals vary widely in their capacity for it. There are some nervous millionaires who never have a moment's leisure, while a really first-class hobo is at leisure nearly all the time. He is blessed with a low sense of obligation and can loaf and invite his soul without getting hives.

Most of us fall, perhaps a bit uncomfortably, between the two extremes. Generally speaking, we know when we have sufficiently discharged our obligations to feel free to do as we damn please for a while—and that's

By E. M. HALLIDAY

always had it. If you live in Marin County,* don't despair. The Greeks and the Persians have some ideas for you

leisure, *ne plus ultra*. It seems like an easy thing, but the pressures of modern civilization are so heavy that it's hard to achieve today—which is something the social scientists ought to be alarmed about more than "too much" leisure. "Feel free" is of the essence; walls may not a prison make, but just the same there's no real leisure under duress. How does one manage to feel free knowing that retaliatory Russian ICBM's are zeroed-in right now on every big American city? Can you feel free from obligation when you know that many of your fellow citizens are alienated from their "unalienable" rights on the totally irrelevant ground of skin color? And what if the work you do for a living strikes you as meaningless or trivial: can six, seven, or eight hours of *that* per day free you for the enjoyment of leisure?

These are hard questions, and they are painfully modern ones for which the experience of the past may be inadequate. More amenable to the light that gleams from history is the subsequent query: what do we want to do with our free time, when the *devoirs* are done and we are truly at leisure? It's no good being free to live deliberately, like Thoreau at Walden, if you can't make up your mind what's worth doing. Lying around doing nothing is no answer; idleness is not idyllic, and a dog's life cannot satisfy a man. Prolonged staring at the television set seems little better—although the contemptuous highbrow remark about "the boob tube" has become one of the more boring clichés.

Leisure and happiness cannot simply be equated, yet in observing that happiness must be pursued the Founding Fathers got near the nut of the problem. In some unarticulated metaphorical way this may explain the attraction that hunting and fishing exert on so many; by a slight extension it may explain the lure of most active sports, including the other kind of venery. Maybe we all have an atavistic nostalgia for that fine Cro-Magnon time when leisure could only mean the aftermath of a good hunt: the belly full, the woman contentedly suckling the child on the bearskin across the cave, firelight flickering against the rocky roof as drowsiness seeped slowly up the spine. The paradoxical joy of camping, which appears to be a form of recreation phenomenally on the rise, is that it playfully imitates the life of primitive man, when it took almost all of everyone's time just to stay alive.

Yet adult play has many nonsporting variants—all of the arts, for instance. "Man is at the most man when his mind is at play," Mark Van Doren once remarked; he was thinking about poetry, which is a play on words. Jean-Louis Barrault, the French actor-director, philosophically justifies his métier in like manner: "*Le jeu est nécessaire à la conservation de l'être humain*," and a play is a chance for the spectator to confront an imaginary situation that he may sometime encounter in real life. If the sounds and

* See page 26

words of the "good" rock music that entrances our children today mean anything, they mean that life is not to be spent foolishly or supinely—"Live your life exactly as you please . . . please . . . please . . . please!" The hedonistic creed, as Ernest Hemingway tried to demonstrate both in his fiction and in his life, can be very serious: it should matter deeply how we spend each single hour of play— for it will never come again. Our Christian fathers expected a Heaven where they would be eternally at leisure after a life of natural hardship here on earth; but few of us are Christians any more in the old sense. There is a lurking suspicion that in that sleep of death that bothered Hamlet, no dreams may come at all.

The essays that follow are by way of taking an eclectic view of what leisure has meant in various cultural environments throughout history—ending with a hard look at American leisure in Marin County, California, a place that seems to epitomize almost too well the current American ideal of the good life. We are calmly setting aside the question of whether there will soon be too much leisure—it may turn out to be an empty question, anyway. How to achieve true leisure, qualitatively, is another matter. Let us consider some intriguing examples.

E. M. Halliday spends his weekend leisure writing articles for Horizon. *Weekdays he labors as Articles Editor for* American Heritage *magazine.*

A Roman mosaic of the fourth century A.D. *shows Plato (third figure from the left) and his disciples conversing in a gymnasium—the courtyard where Greek youths took exercise and where philosophy was born.*

Greeks and Romans at their Ease

The classical world discovered the two classic ways to stay amused: exercising one's mind or benumbing it

Rich people have always had leisure, and most of them have always used it for the same occupations: killing animals and birds, collecting beautiful women and other works of art, building large houses and filling them with useless but decorative equipment, eating and drinking, and working out systems of social differentiation almost as elaborate as the intestines of a computer. Ordinary people have always had festivals: a time to relax after getting in the harvest, a dance and a few drinks after making the new wine, a big blast to kick out the old year and welcome in the new—all usually tied up with religion, so that a holy day is a holiday.

As far as I know, the Jews were the first people to introduce, not simply seasonal festivals, but regular periods of leisure for everybody, rich and poor alike. Once every seven days, on the Sabbath, "thou shalt not do any work, thou, nor thy son, nor thy daughter," and the commandment goes on through the servants and the livestock and even the visitors from outside. This is real leisure: a blessed day of rest. Later the rule was extended, and the Jews were commanded not only to do no work on the Sabbath, but to enjoy it: wear their best clothes, eat three meals, and rejoice. It is a great gift, the Sabbath.

However, it was the classical Greeks who took the idea of general free-floating leisure and improved it by thinking of something to do that was quite different from work. They invented the gymnasium. The word and the idea "athlete" are both Greek. Nowadays we are apt to think of the Greeks as brilliant thinkers and agile conversationalists, but many of them were handsome bodies with much spirit and grace and not a great deal of brain. Everyone who goes to Delphi and sees the bronze charioteer is charmed by the skill of the sculptor and disappointed by the expressionless face of the young man whose victory he commemorated. But this is correct. The Greeks founded the Olympic games in 776 B.C., long before a single philosopher opened his mouth.

"Health is best," begins one of their drinking songs, which does not even mention intelligence. Healthiest and stupidest of all were the Spartans. They did no work at all, ever. They hunted in the rugged mountains and exercised and drilled for the next war and sat around talking laconically, while the Helots whom they had conquered worked on the farms.

The gymnasium was a Greek solution to the problem of leisure. But it became something more than a training school for young athletes and an exercise area for the middle-aged. A Greek who did not have to work all day on his farm or sell goods in a shop gravitated to the gymnasium. The Greeks loved talking, and some Greeks were highly intelligent; so, as they sat in the gymnasium, resting between bouts of physical training or watching the youngsters leap and wrestle, they exchanged ideas. In time the gymnasium became a club, in which serious matters were discussed. It came to embody that fine balance between body and mind that was the best product of Greece. Socrates would often sit in a sunny corner questioning the young men in order to make their minds as supple as their muscles. Greek education kept growing more elaborate. A library was added to the gymnasium, teachers of literature joined the staff, classes were systematized, and what had at one time been a place in which men of leisure could run and jump and take sunbaths grew into a school.

School is a Greek word, scholé. If a Greek was really poor, he had to help his father on the farm, grubbing up roots and watching the goats. If he had a little extra cash, he went to the place of leisure.

The Romans were originally not much for leisure. They were too busy conquering the world. This was not primarily an imperialistic plan. It was the expression of their driving restlessness and their built-in love of challenge and difficulty and effort. Work, fight, serve, work, save, plan, work. Old Cato objected bitterly to the time people spent standing around yakking in the Forum: he wanted it paved with sharp-edged shells. Like other Romans he despised the Greeks for wasting hours every day oiling their bodies and wrestling, and oiling their tongues and arguing. Why didn't they get together and build a few decent roads and bridges and aqueducts? They are still there, the great Roman highways, and they symbolize the republican Romans' belief that wasting time and avoiding hard work was a sin.

Rome started out poor and had to work. Rome became rich—so rich that for many of its people work was a waste of time. As the conquest of the world was completed, the small subsistence farmers had their land swallowed up by big landholders; the long-term soldiers were discharged with nothing to do; floating populations from all over the empire drifted into the big cities with no real trade or skill to guarantee them a steady livelihood. Under the republic the city-dwelling Romans worked hard. Under the emperors they worked less and less. Not only Rome but the other big centers, Alexandria and Antioch and many more, were full of surplus

By GILBERT HIGHET

people who had to be fed and amused. The government was forced to provide free food and amusement for this mass leisure. Juvenal called the solution "bread and circuses."

Food was a problem of agriculture, transport, and economics, and it would take a large book to describe how the Roman officials tried to solve it. (Food tickets, extra handouts of oil and wine and sometimes cash, but no guaranteed income.) Once the Romans had adopted the idea of leisure, they arranged it with efficient vulgarity through three large-scale institutions. These institutions satisfied basic human impulses: physical exercise and comfort, competition, and hunting.

Much leisure was spent in the huge public baths: exercising, being massaged, showering, playing handball, swimming, and sun-bathing—and also gambling, chatting, strolling, looking at the exhibitions of paintings and statues, and occasionally listening to poets reciting their own works. The Roman baths were projections of the Greek gymnasiums into a more affluent era: they were superclubs. Admission was a few cents only. Did it matter if you slept in a six-story walkup if you could spend most of the day in an establishment that would have made a Hilton hotel look like a slum?

The Romans also loved to watch men kill animals and one another. The same impulse that makes Arab sheiks in air-conditioned Cadillacs run down gazelles and butcher them with machine guns made the Romans enjoy seeing men grapple with wild beasts in the arena. The modern descendant of the Roman beast hunt is the Spanish bullfight, in which there can be no satisfaction without a killing. *Arena* is the Latin word for sand; and the sand, like the eyes of the spectators, will soak up blood of beast or man without discrimination.

One of the great spectacles was a hunt. Strange imported animals were driven into the circus (sometimes prepared as a jungle with exotic trees and bushes), and trained hunters tried to capture or kill them. A single man would face a lion. A woman alone would tackle a wild boar. The emperor Commodus personally killed five hippopotamuses and two elephants in two days; one of his stunts was beheading ostriches from the imperial box with a broad-bladed arrow. (The disgusting trick of tying up criminals and setting animals to devour them was a late invention, based on Gresham's law that bad shows drive out good.)

Gladiators—the word means "swordsmen," and a gladiolus is a little sword—were originally war prisoners sacrificed at the funeral of the general who captured them. They fought one another to the death—a more honorable fate than being passively butchered—and their blood fed his spirit. This was the one practice, among the many cruelties and vulgarities of the Romans, that other nations despised most bitterly. But the Romans were rich and powerful, and subject peoples wished to please them, and so the habit spread. Even in the theatre of Dionysus at Athens, where men had once staged noble tragedies to honor the god, trained fighters killed each other, so that the blood splashed the front seats and the distinguished spectators who sat in them. After the emperor Trajan conquered what is now Rumania, he brought back many millions of dollars' worth of gold and booty. He gave Rome public shows that lasted for 117 days of honorific leisure. Nearly five thousand pairs of gladiators were pitted against each other, while the crowds roared.

Horse races were seldom run as they are now, with single horses ridden by jockeys. Each entry was a group of four horses yoked to a light chariot and driven by a skilled charioteer. This was the only spectator sport in antiquity organized by teams. Each team had special horses, stables, drivers, supporters, and colors: red, white, green, blue. The sillier Roman emperors would wear the colors of their favorite team and even sleep in the stables with the drivers. After Christian Rome was founded in Constantinople, the horse races continued there amid wild enthusiasm. Disputes between fan clubs grew into large-scale disorders. During the WIN WIN WIN riots in A.D. 532 the powerful emperor Justinian was besieged in his palace, the cathedral of the Holy Wisdom was burned down, and for five days the mob ruled the city.

Magnificent public baths, savage animals killed by hunters for show; the Colosseum filled with water so that sea battles could be staged to amuse the public; expert swordsmen fighting duels, and in the lunch interval criminals sent in with swords but without armor, to kill each other off as quickly and bloodily as possible; chariot races; and always the yelling mobs. These were the occupations of mass leisure in the Roman Empire.

Where did Roman culture come from, then? It came from the gymnasium and not from the arena. The Greeks founded Western civilization and taught the Romans how to use it. In mind, the greatest Romans were half-Greek. They exercised their bodies, but they developed their minds in leisure. They had nothing but loathing, or at most patient contempt, for the races and the beast hunts and the blood on the sand. The Greeks created an almost complete civilization of the spirit. The Romans have left us a tradition of law and politics, some splendid public architecture, and several hundred fine books written by men in quiet rooms from which they could scarcely hear the voice of the many-headed beast in the circus roaring WIN WIN WIN! Leisure, for the mass, is a narcotic or an intoxicant. For the thoughtful man leisure is the Sabbath in which he can have a conversation with his soul.

Gilbert Highet is Anthon Professor of Latin Language and Literature and Chairman of the department of Greek and Latin at Columbia University.

The gladiator at bottom has been slain by his sword-bearing adversary, and "Cupido," at top, is about to be dispatched. Such is the spectator sport depicted in this fourth-century Roman mosaic.

In this painting from the Sung dynasty (A.D. 960–1279) five bearded scholar-officials, attended by servants, use their leisure to collate ancient texts in the outdoor pavilion of a private house.

Learned Bureaucrats in China

To be a connoisseur can fill the hours of a whole lifetime

There was never a social class quite like the scholar-officials of imperial China—the calm, Confucian gentlemen known as mandarins, who were at one and the same time the administrators of a vast empire and the most meticulous connoisseurs of its ancient culture. Here were men who might spend their office hours managing the granaries of a province and their leisure time arranging rocks in their gardens or inditing essays on the virtues of their favorite kinds of inkstone. So well blended in the mandarins were the scholar and the administrator that, of the eighty-eight leading literary figures formally recognized in China's Tang dynasty (A.D. 618–907), all but three were government officials.

Strictly speaking, the cherished avocations of these scholar-officials should not, perhaps, be called leisure activities in the sense of pursuits wholly unconnected with work. It was precisely because a Chinese scholar was a scholar that he could become a public official, and it was because he was steeped in Chinese literature and art that he was held fit to govern. That political theory originated with Confucius, and it was based on his revolutionary doctrine that only men of the highest ethical spirit had a right to rule. This ethical spirit, Confucius taught in the sixth century B.C., could be acquired only through studying the great examples of ancient wisdom and virtue found in Chinese literature and history. In time the classical canon came to include not only the most ancient texts but, pre-eminently, the classical Confucian writings themselves, and the entire range of Chinese high culture.

The institutional embodiment of this Confucian ideal was the famed imperial civil service examinations, which predated those of the West by more than a millennium. A young man who aspired to become an official was required to pass a literary test given every few years in his local district. In it he was asked to write a highly formal composition on some ethical aspect of the Four Books of Confucianism. If he passed, he not only became eligible for a provincial post, he passed out of the realm of ordinary men, for a scholar in China enjoyed enormous prestige; men in his native village would prize samples of his autograph. To enter the national bureaucracy he had to pass a more severe test given at the provincial level. Should he aspire in his ripe years to the higher offices of state, he had still to pass the awesome metropolitan examinations that were held in Peking.

The scholar who actually became an official was supposed to be a man of the world, not a drudge. As the old mandarin saying went: "The accomplished scholar is not a utensil." He usually held his office hours in the morning, and in addition to his free afternoons and his holidays he was given a three-year leave upon the death of his father for meditation and pursuit of his avocations. As a great sixteenth-century Chinese painter (and official) observed: "The cultivated man in retirement from office frequently takes pleasure in playing with the brush and producing landscapes for his own gratification."

The variety of learned hobbies was considerable. Amateur archaeology, for example, was a favored pastime among scholar-officials, who enjoyed the search for bronze ritual vessels, stones, and steles, highly prized for the examples of ancient inscriptions they might afford. Much scholarship went into the study of these finds. As one admiring official wrote about another: "He was capable of dating all vases and bells of the Hsia and Shang periods." After the sixteenth century a great vogue among scholar-officials was the collecting and collating of finely printed books, a hobby pursued so intensively that many wealthy families went bankrupt supporting the bibliomania of their kinsmen.

Yet the scholar-official did not need wealth to cultivate his ease. He always had his little garden plot—its smallness, perhaps, a point of pride—in which to arrange, as artfully as he could, some odd-shaped rocks he had found by the wayside or acquired in a swap. More to the point, he always had the "Four Precious Things of the Scholar's Table": inkstone, ink sticks, brush, and paper or silk. With them he could be a painter, a writer, a calligrapher, with all of Chinese culture to emulate or imitate; to make a perfect copy of a classic work was not thought a dubious activity by the Chinese. If the scholar lacked any special creative ability, he could devote grave care to these tools themselves, perfecting some special ink, preparing a superior inkstone or paper—for the willingness to take infinite pains with small things was a particular characteristic of the scholar-official. In a sense the mandarin system provided a suitable hobby for gentlemen of every taste and temperament. As long as a man's pursuits were linked to the cultural tradition of his ancestors, they had a dignity and prestige recognized by all. Perhaps it is only under the conditions provided by this dominant Confucian outlook that a system of leisure based on the pursuit of cultural hobbies could have succeeded.

By WALTER KARP

13

Il Trebbio, near Florence, one of several Medici villas, was Lorenzo's hunting lodge. The house and quattro-cento gardens, still to be seen today, are here depicted by the seventeenth-century Italian painter Giusto Utens.

The Pursuit of Happiness in a Villa

To the aristocrat of the Italian Renaissance, leisure was anything but restful

The Oxford English Dictionary in defining "leisure" gives to this word, in addition to its common significance of "free time," another meaning: "Time allowed before it is too late." In this sense the Renaissance man had an acute appreciation of the value of leisure. In the Middle Ages people had had rather too much time to spare: the monk in his cell, the peasant bound by the rhythm of the seasons, the lady immured in her castle. But for the Renaissance man, as for the Greek, life was too short for his manifold activities. "Cosimo" (de' Medici), wrote Marsilio Ficino, "was as avaricious of his time as Midas was of gold." When forming the library for the Badia Fiesolana, he engaged no fewer than forty-five copyists, who produced two hundred volumes in twenty-two months. The ambassador Giannozzo Manetti slept only five hours a night during his five years in Florence and could not even once spare the time to cross the Arno. Leon Battista Alberti —architect, classicist, mathematician, musician, astronomer, poet—believed that "man is born to work at magnificent tasks on a vast scale, thus pleasing and honoring God." He designed for himself an emblem: an eye beneath a falcon's wing (because of "the sharpness of its vision and the strength of its wings")—an image of the union of supreme insight and supreme power. Beneath it he inscribed the Ciceronian formula "*Quid tum?*"—"What then?"

What then, indeed; what next? The Renaissance man was always on the brink of discovery: his astronomers and cartographers produced new maps of both the earth and skies, his explorers discovered a new continent in the West, his scholars brought back from the East the means to revive classical learning and art. And he himself aspired not only to equal the achievements of the Greeks and Romans but also to attain, through a reconciliation of Platonic philosophy with Christian faith, a vision of complete harmony based on "the beauty of the spirit and of *all* its fruits"—since, to Marsilio Ficino as to Plato, beauty and good were one and Platonic love their highest human expression. Thence the importance attached by the Renaissance man to friendship, since, according to Ficino, "in such a relationship there are always at least three partners: two

Alberti's emblem was this "winged eye," a symbol of man's insight and power.

human beings, and God, who founded their friendship."

Friendships such as these, however, can only exist within a framework of leisure: time deliberately devoted to the intercourse of what Milton called "fit conversing souls." To achieve this, it was necessary to leave the city and all its cares—and thus the Renaissance villa came into being.

Not that, even before this, the Tuscan had been unaware of the charms of country life and of its security. During the Great Plague of 1348, when every house was filled with the dying and the streets resounded to the cry "Bring out your dead!" the characters of Boccaccio's *Decameron* spent their days in various villas of the neighborhood (one being the Villa Palmieri near San Domenico, and one

Poggio Gherardo at Settignano); and there, in green gardens filled with birds and streams, they cast off their fears by telling stories and closed each day with dancing and a song.

A century later Alberti's panegyric on country life reveals an awareness not only of pleasures offered by the land but of its bounty. "In the spring the villa bestows infinite solace upon you: greenery, flowers, scent and song: all things smile at you and hold promise of a good harvest. And how courteous you find it in summer! . . . It sends you first one fruit and then another, never is the house denied its liberality. And here comes the autumn . . . and in return for a little sweat, more and more barrels of wine, and it fills your house with nuts, pears and sweet apples. Even in winter, the villa does not forget to be liberal: it sends you wood and oil, and juniper and laurel, to comfort you when you come home out of the snow and wind, with a gay and scented flame . . . Here you may live in peace, feeding your little family, and holding converse about oxen, wool, vines and seeds. No enemy, no hate, no malevolence arise from cultivating one's own fields. O God, it is a true Paradise."

Alberti's own paradise, plainly, is a modest one, but that which he plans for his great patrons, the Medici, is on a grander scale. His ideas are fully set down in his treatise *De Re Aedificatoria* (1459). The house, he says, should be placed on a hillside, "with a fine view over the plain and familiar hill-tops" and, close by, "the delight of gardens." The loggia should be sunny in winter, shady in summer: the avenues lined by trees symmetrically planted, pomegranates or cherries, and garlanded with roses. There must be fountains surrounded by flower vases, as in the gardens of Alexandria and Agrigentum, grottoes like those described by Ovid; and pergolas of vines supported on marble pillars should lead into a "secret garden," in which box hedges enclose sweet flowers and aromatic herbs. Another garden, described in the *Hypnerotomachia*, an allegorical romance by Francesco Colonna (1467), contained a rose garden planted only with the varieties mentioned by Pliny. Moreover Lorenzo de' Medici and the archaeologist Braccio Bracciolini also adorned their gardens with classical statues, while Lorenzo added an Ionic portico and frieze to his villa at Poggio a Caiano. In all this the classical influence was deliberate, since the main purpose of these villas was to provide a setting favorable for meditation, philosophy, and the study of the arts. "Yesterday," wrote Cosimo de' Medici to Ficino in the last months of his life, "I came to the villa of Careggi, not to cultivate my fields, but my soul . . . Bring our Plato's book *Concerning the Highest Good* . . . I desire nothing so much as to know the best road to happiness—Farewell, and do not come without the Orphean lyre."

In the Careggi gardens three generations of the Medici (Cosimo, Piero, Lorenzo) gathered around them the greatest thinkers and artists of their time: Marsilio Ficino, Pico della Mirandola, Leonardo Bruni, Poliziano, Brunelleschi, Michelozzo, Donatello, and the young Michelangelo, whom already at thirteen Lorenzo treated "with much respect." Here they discussed the dominant themes of the day: the nature of beauty, honor, love, nobility, riches, the liberal arts. And should astrology be considered a true science, and was "natural magic," as opposed to necromancy, permissible? What should one make of that strange letter from the explorer Columbus, about which a song was being sung in the Florentine streets? Was action or contemplation the highest purpose of man's life? And what was the essence of the dignity of man? And then, as

the shadows lengthened, Lorenzo and his friends would sometimes ride up the Fiesole hill to the pleasure villa that Michelozzo had built for him, to spend the evening in the garden overlooking the Florentine plain, in dancing or singing or making love. "*Chi vuol esser lieto sia—Di doman non c'è certezza*" ("Take joy upon the wing—Tomorrow holds no certainty").

The prototype of the Renaissance man, Lorenzo had been granted almost every gift that his contemporaries valued: vigor of body, strength of passions, skill in every sport, wisdom

COLL. OF THE CONTESSA SOFIA BOSSI PUCCI SERRISTORI

In the evenings Machiavelli put on his best robes, as this portrait shows, and entered the "courts of the ancients."

in statesmanship and in the management of his international bank. What use did he make of his leisure? He made love, bred horses, read Plato, collected statues and precious stones, wrote poetry, designed buildings, danced, hunted, played with his children, and accompanied his own poems upon the lyre, "as if possessed by a divine fury." But he was not a happy man. Too many of the tensions of the age were reflected in him: the conflict between his civic duties and his longing for a sensual Bacchic existence, between the active and the contemplative life, between the pagan and the Christian worlds, seeking a God he

could not find. "If amid riches, honors and pleasures I seek Thee, Lord, the more I look, the less I find Thee."

One other instance of country leisure must also be given: that described by Niccolò Machiavelli in a letter from his small villa at S. Andrea in Percussina, to which he had retired after being accused of having conspired against the Medici. He relates how, after rising with the sun and spending a couple of hours with his woodcutters, he settles down in his fowling hut. "I have a book with me, either Dante or Petrarch or one of those minor poets such as Tibullus and Ovid. I read about their passions and their loves; I remember my own, and for a short while this makes me happy." In the afternoon he plays backgammon in the inn with the innkeeper, a butcher, and two bakers, and they come to words about a farthing, "yet our shouts can be heard as far as San Casciano." But then, "when evening comes, I return home and go into my study. On the threshold I strip off my muddy, sweaty, workday clothes and put on the robes of court and palace, and in this graver dress I enter the antique courts of the ancients, and there I taste the food that alone is mine, and for which I was born. And there I make bold to speak to them and ask the motives for their actions, and they, in their humanity, reply to me. And for the space of four hours I forget the world, remember no vexation, fear poverty no more, tremble no more at death: I pass indeed into their world. And as Dante says that there can be no understanding unless the memory retains what it has heard, I have written down what I have gained from their conversation, and composed a small work, *De principatibus*." Thus, in those evenings of country leisure, a book that molded the art of statesmanship for four centuries, *The Prince*, was set down.

Iris Origo, the distinguished biographer and social historian, formerly lived in the Medici villa at Fiesole.

Above, young men and women beguile the hours outdoors in this detail of a fourteenth-century fresco, thought to be by Andrea Orcagna. Below, in a garden of northern Italy lords and ladies enjoy a snowball fight in an anonymous fresco.

Flowers in bloom, dancing girls, music, wine, fruit, and a lovely companion were the pleasures of this Persian prince. A court artist painted this garden of delights around 1533.

Persian Diversions

Did they really live that way? Well, yes

Some pleasures glow more brightly in retrospect, or vicariously. This may be true of the traditional Persian pleasures, at least as we know them from the art of the Persian miniature; but whether those colors are authentically fresh or wishfully touched up, no more beguiling image of the leisure arts has ever been presented—ivory-clear, crystal, with tiny etched figures in attitudes of sensual repose, with little blue birds in limpid skies, with fountains and girls and gazebos. The Persians, in their sixteenth- and seventeenth-century heyday, had refined the austerities of Islam into philosophic and artistic forms of delicate subtlety, and nowhere more fastidiously than in the practice of pleasure.

They were prodded into those enviable postures by history and environment. They were flower people before their time. Once the masters of the world, they had been humiliated by the conquering Arabs; caged in a harsh, gigantic landscape, they yearned for gentle and seductive things. Their mystic poets had preached the merits of escape, the delusion of worldly achievement, the transience of success. Their artists specialized in secrecy, reduction, and surprise; enclaves, contrasts, green against dun, small beside enormous, coolness in the desert. With national glory discredited, individual worth became the measure of distinction, and cultured hospitality was a patriotic habit.

Did they really sit in those delectable gardens exchanging verses and sipping the wines of Shiraz? Yes. If we cannot believe every quatrain or brushstroke of the Persians themselves, we have the evidence of foreigners to go by. The garden was the center of their pleasures. It was formal in design, profuse in character. We hear of paths strewn thick with plucked roses, blossoms floating in garden pools, violets of many colors, kiosks whose elaborate roofs mirrored the play of the water beneath. Doves swirled through the poplars, fish lazed deep in marble tanks; here we see a musician at his instrument, and there the little Shah Abbas II, ten years old, solemnly balances oranges from a silver dish upon the jet of an ornamental fountain.

These were altogether sensual *divertissements*, and essentially outdoor. It was in the garden that the Persians entertained, preferably with a light spring shower falling outside the summerhouse, to lay the dust and bring out the flower scents. Poetic fancy infused it all. Then as now, the lyrics of the classical Persian poets were known to every educated man and influenced every Persian taste. Relax, they seemed to sing; come into the shade, listen to the waters and the birds:

> This world is all cloud and storm,
>   A tear, a sigh:
> Pour the wine then, and let
>   The world pass by.

Women were always in the garden. Islam had not abased the old urbanity of the Persians, and though women were shut away from public view, their purdah was not all stuffiness. Within the high walls they moved, it seems, merrily enough: one shah used to sit on a throne in the center of a pool while the ladies of his harem, one by one, slid helter-skelter down a chute from a gallery into his lascivious embrace. The girls of the miniatures generally have a winsome look, but perhaps it is just vertiginous.

There was wine, too, *pace* the quibbling scholars who maintain that Omar Khayyám was a puritanical moralist all the time. Islam might call wine "an abomination," and the poets may sometimes have been singing metaphorically, but wine was still made in Persia by Zoroastrians and foreigners, and it was never absent from Persian leisure hours. "It is incredible," wrote Dr. John Fryer of England in 1698, "to see what Quantities they drink at a Merry-meeting, and how unconcerned the next day they appear." According to John Chardin, who was in Persia in the 1670's, the wine of Kazvin was "*le plus violent du monde*," but on the other hand it never needed to be corked: so pure was the atmosphere that one had only to stick a carnation in the bottle neck to keep the contents fresh and sparkling.

For though the Persian pleasures were, like the pleasures of most ages, basically wine, women, and song, they were touched with the delicate precision of imagination, almost Japanese, that has always been the glory of Persia. Today the old gardens are mostly overgrown and tumble-down, Persian architecture has long since gone to seed, and wine is not often drunk to poetry in rose bowers. But some of the charm survives to be a lesson to us all —in the love of words, for instance, the piquant bubbling humor of intercourse; or in the innocent sophistication of a Persian salad, like a little green poem itself, its meadow herbs grouped artlessly around a lyric of cucumber, or the central inspiration of a radish.

James Morris's travels have resulted in several articles for Horizon. *His most recent contribution, however, was a story on his homeland, Wales, which appeared in the Winter issue.*

By JAMES MORRIS

The racing of horses, a gentleman's pleasure in old England, came to be an organized sport in the eighteenth century and a mass spectacle in the nineteenth. This jockey and his mount were painted by James Seymour around 1750.

The Beginnings of Modern Pleasures

In eighteenth-century England the games of kings began to be accessible to all

Of course, people have often been idle, and they have always had holidays. Even in the darkest days of the Dark Ages the rich hunted, jousted, sang, danced, and made love. The peasants gorged, got drunk, cavorted about their maypoles.

Yet true leisure must have its obverse—regular and acknowledged hours of work. And this requires a highly sophisticated commercial and industrial society. The agrarian world does not know leisure in our sense. One has only to compare India with America to grasp this obvious point. Hence, for many centuries leisure activities were confined to the great cities with their strong merchant class or to the rich court circles that needed to dispel boredom. Many of the pleasurable pastimes of courts and cities, including some that had a utilitarian content, passed into the world of leisure. Men of the sixteenth and seventeenth centuries raced horses not only because they loved a bet and enjoyed the invigorating gallop, but also because they wanted to improve the breed. Similarly, hunting the stag or fox was good practice for a cavalry charge. Even the rural sports—archery, wrestling, prize fighting—had their military uses.

Most of the games that we enjoy have their origins in the need to train the male body, to teach it quick co-ordination of eye and muscle and make it capable of endurance under hostile conditions. But how vast is the distance from a group of peasants in an English village fighting and kicking to gain possession of an inflated pig's bladder to the highly organized football teams of the American college campus! This is a change of momentous significance and one that has affected all the amusements and pas-times that beguile mankind.

If we look backward to rural Elizabethan England, we find a different world of leisure. Sports and amusements of course existed, but they were either very personal or deeply embedded in religious or social ritual. When the harvest demanded it, rich and poor, young and old, joined in and worked throughout the daylight hours; the harvest home, they rejoiced, thanked God in their churches, danced, feasted, and got drunk; even, like any pagan, making offerings of corn to their God, who had been kind. Work and rejoicing intermingled.

The rich were forced to fill their own leisure hours as best they might, hunting, riding, fishing, shooting, or looking forward to the visit of a wandering minstrel or a gang of strolling players. Sometimes they organized dances in their halls and barns; festivities lasted for days, until food and drink or guests were exhausted. If they were culturally inclined, they collected and read books and listened to interminable sermons. If very rich they might indulge in ostentation, decorating their houses with paintings and rich furnishings. But all of these activities had social overtones. The festivities in the manor house were partly political, for they cemented neighborhood alliances. The ostentation of culture was designed to make rank and affluence visible. Even the richest of men, the most noble of aristocrats, did not conceive of themselves as leisured. They might withdraw from the world, but not in order to be idle. In retirement they exercised their bodies, improved their minds, or cultivated their souls.

The same is true for women: indeed, only a few women about the courts of princes or in the upper classes of the cities were really leisured in our sense. The ordinary noble-woman or gentlewoman throughout Europe was active during the day managing her household, from the marking of linen to the baking of bread. For relaxation her women might sing to her or read to her from a romance.

Perceptible changes in the varieties and functions of leisure began in the last quarter of the seventeenth century and gathered momentum in the eighteenth, becoming an avalanche in the nineteenth century. England led the way not only because it was rich but also because it possessed in London a huge metropolis and a large and growing pseudo gentry or upper middle class: that is, men and women who were rich enough to live without working, yet lacked the burden of estates, or whose professional careers gave them regular hours and regular leisure. Furthermore the gentry and aristocracy became rich enough to use professionally trained men to run their estates for them. With acres of time to be filled, leisure slowly but steadily became an industry, and one of enormous potential profit, requiring capital investment, systematized techniques, active marketing, and creative ingenuity; leisure got the lot.

Take horse racing. In the seventeenth century it was largely a matter of two gentlemen adjourning to a nearby heath, fixing a wager, and riding their horses against each other; sometimes their neighbors would turn up and they would all race, one against the other, until the winner eliminated the rest. Since King James I loved hunting, and Newmarket possessed wonderful open turf, the court adjourned there; local aristocrats flocked in, and days of wagering, racing, and

LE QOQUE EN PATE

Rowlandson

Thomas Rowlandson, a merciless observer of his countrymen at play, made this etching in 1810, showing some English travelers in

drinking followed. By the end of the seventeenth century regular meetings were emerging, and professional riders—jockeys—had begun to establish themselves, although many owners still rode their own mounts. There were few or no rules. Jockeys tried to unseat each other at the start of the race and used their whips on each other as much as on their horses.

As betting grew, races multiplied, and the need for some sort of regulation became pressing. A governing body for racing, the Jockey Club, was founded about 1750. Rules were laid down, race meetings were properly organized, and public stands built. Entries were controlled; race horses were increasingly bred with carefully kept pedigrees. The Racing Calendar officially recorded all race meetings and winners. Gentlemen might still bet against each other, but now bookmakers catered to the general public. Within a hundred years racing had developed into an organized public spectacle drawing huge crowds to the

France setting out by coach from a French inn

considerable fortunes for themselves and their patrons. Boxing was still a savage sport fought without gloves, but at least accepted rules were established in 1743. In cricket, too, an ancient game, rules were codified in the eighteenth century. Lasting for hours, sometimes for days, cricket was a middle-class sport played by gentlemen or their servants or by innkeepers and farmers taking a day's leisure; it attracted both noble patrons and much betting as well.

Soccer, the game of the peasants and workers, did not become organized and a public spectacle until the nineteenth century, when the working classes first obtained a little weekend leisure. The process was twofold: eager public participation turned amateur sporting activities into highly professional organized games involving stadiums, capital, and traditions of all kinds. The road to Santa Anita, Madison Square Garden, and the Houston Astrodome had been started.

It was not only in games that leisure became a profitable industry: sport and betting do not attract everyone all the time, least of all women. We like to think of ourselves today as being in the midst of a startling cultural explosion. It began with quite considerable rumblings more than two centuries ago. In mid-seventeenth century London, Paris, or Madrid there were no picture galleries, no concerts, no cheap prints, no circulating libraries; most books were theological, with a sprinkling of volumes of poetry, romance, and travel. There were no newspapers apart from official gazettes, no literary magazines, no clubs nor assembly rooms.

If you wished to see pictures, you had to dress in the finery of gentility and visit the court or bribe the housekeeper of a nobleman. If you loved music, you went to church or played it with friends. If avid for news you subscribed to a private newsletter. If convivial you organized a dance in your own home. If bookish you developed a taste for theology or history. Culture was personal or the affair of a narrow, rich, and generally aristocratic social class. London provided a few pleasures: sight-seeing—one or two moth-eaten lions and tigers at the Tower or exhibits of gifts from Eastern potentates—a couple of theatres, great numbers of whores, and endless taverns. Genteel places of amusement scarcely existed. And this was true of most of the capital cities of Europe.

A hundred years later all was changed, and again England, with its ever-increasing prosperous middle class, led the way. Concerts were now a commonplace, as well as opera and ballet. The Royal Academy, founded in 1768, provided a yearly feast of art, but, better still for the growing culture-minded public, artists secured a copyright for engravings of their pictures by an act of Parliament passed in 1735. William Hogarth leaped in at once, and soon handsome etchings of his masterpieces—*Marriage à la Mode, A Rake's Progress,* etc.—were festooning the walls of middle-class houses, along with the famous beauties of Joshua Reynolds or Thomas Gainsborough. The British Museum came into being in 1753, the very first of the great metropolitan museums. By the third quarter of the eighteenth century all forms of art and learning were at a premium.

From the days of Addison's *Spectator,* in the early 1700's, literary journals had waxed and waned, but always multiplied. Newspapers to fill the idle hours in the morning or evening were everywhere available. Circulating libraries and book subscription clubs were started near the middle of the century and soon spread throughout the land: even remote country towns had their book clubs, assembly rooms, and debating societies. The novel, an all but nonexistent literary form in the seventeenth century, flooded the bookshops throughout the eighteenth. Lectures and schools for adult learners

great classic meetings—the St. Leger, established in 1776, the Oaks in 1779, and the Derby in 1780.

As with horse racing, so with prize fighting: instead of village blacksmiths clouting each other for a wager, it became an organized sport with national champions who performed before huge crowds and made abounded in London and the provincial towns. Dancing academies did not rely only on the young, for the middle-aged flocked to them, too.

Consumer spending is, par excellence, a leisure activity, and every foreigner who came to London in the eighteenth century was amazed by the shop windows with their elegant displays. The world flocked to Josiah Wedgwood's showrooms, where his latest patterns were displayed on tables laid for dinner. The art of selling—advertising, puffing, displaying with every trick of light—developed rapidly, sustained by a growing leisure class that could shop and shop and shop. There was money in culture, money in literature, money in diversions. If we have become jaded with the consumer society that seems to spend its free time devouring the world's goods, we must remember that to the English men and women of the eighteenth century the new abundance was novel and exciting: spending on the fineries of life was almost as intoxicating as gambling.

As the demand for consumer goods grew in volume, inventors found cheap substitutes—in the way that plastics are used today—for what the mass of the people wanted but could not afford. Artificial stone—Coade—was invented so that the middle class could have what appeared to be a stone facing to their houses, while the development of the silver plating process enabled them to deck their tables like the rich. Adornment and display require time: time to acquire the finery and, above all, time to show it off. Without leisure it is impossible to keep up with the Joneses. But the Joneses started their reckless consumer binge 'way back in eighteenth-century England.

The dangers of leisure, as the upper classes of nineteenth-century England soon learned, are boredom and guilt. A change of scene, it was quickly discovered, provided a sovereign remedy for tedium. In earlier ages few had traveled for fun, the conditions of roads and inns being too barbarous. By 1750 the upper classes were on the move—to Scotland, Ireland, France, Italy, even Russia and Turkey. Inns improved, entrepreneurs produced guidebooks, maps, coach-rental agencies; except for cheap package tours, the whole paraphernalia of modern travel was available by 1800. And towns were growing that were devoted entirely to the pursuit of leisure.

True, the lingering sense of guilt that hinted of the immorality of idleness required an excuse. Travel was justified as improving the mind. Health provided the reason for a prolonged stay at a spa or seaside resort. The waters of Bath were famous, and a visit to the Pump Room soothed the conscience amid the balls, assemblies, plays, the ogling, love-making, and gambling that made up a day there. Everyone who could afford it swarmed to Bath for—although they would not admit it—a holiday. Scores of spas copying Bath sprang into life—Tunbridge Wells, Harrogate, Malvern, and a host of minor ones now forgotten. And when Dr. Richard Russell sold the idea of sea bathing as a route to health, Brighton quietly became the eighteenth-century Miami, a tiny village burgeoning into a town based purely on visitors and retired residents. There, oddly enough, men and women bathed in the nude, although segregated, and many gentlemen spent a happy morning viewing beauties through their telescopes. This was the beginning of Atlantic City and Laguna Beach and Saint-Tropez, of that endless array of communities that stretches along the coasts of the civilized world, providing delectation for the leisured and profit for those who exploit them.

Meanwhile, moralists, not the least of whom was Hogarth, were quick to stress that the road to the gallows often begins with idleness or a love of the luxuries of leisure. Preachers knew that idle hands would rove, that men and women with time on their hands would turn to their sofas, then regarded as a danger to morals. And they recognized well enough that the business of pornography was growing by leaps and bounds. Many deplored the vulgarization that leisure brought, the commercialization of the arts, the exploitation of sensibility for economic ends. The worm was in the bud, even in the first riotous enjoyment of a leisured world. Then as now, the pursuit of leisure was accompanied by a chorus of Jeremiahs who prophesied the decay of national and family morality. However, its love of leisure did not prevent Britain from beating Napoleon's France.

Of course, the serious-minded and idiosyncratic rejected public amusements and avoided the pleasures of the herd. They used their free time to cultivate their own gardens. With leisure comes the vast proliferation of hobbies, the extension of collecting from accumulating a grab bag of curiosities to highly specialized and professional concentration. And men and women, not merely aristocrats, had time to cultivate their own personalities, to turn themselves into works of art. Eccentricity, like exhibitionism, is released in a leisured world. Only the idle rich can easily be themselves.

Perhaps the greatest of all social revolutions—and one of enormous economic consequences, as yet scarcely explored—began in the eighteenth century, when Europe not only grew rich enough to support a large class of nonworkers, but also began to organize the days of those who toiled into hours of work and hours of leisure: from that moment the former was bound to diminish and the latter to grow. Leisure had come to stay; man was at last on his way to turning his world into a playground.

Professor of Modern English History at the University of Cambridge, J. H. Plumb was elected this past year to membership in the British Academy.

A cheerful, motley crowd places its bets at Epsom Downs in this detail from W. P. Frith's Derby Day. *By 1857, when the painting was begun, playing the horses had become a public pastime.*

A Few Hazards of the Good Life

The contemporary version of the earthly paradise may be unfit for human habitation

Across the Golden Gate, in the County of Marin, opposite San Francisco, there are 4,000 acres of some of the most beautiful coastline in California. The scenic and historic splendor of the acreage so near to a great city is unrivaled anywhere . . .   —CALIFORNIA DIVISION OF PARKS AND RECREATION

A few weeks ago, in the course of a conversation with a man who runs an institute for treating alcoholics, I asked where the greatest incidence of alcoholism occurs in the San Francisco area, which is notoriously one of the wettest places in the world. My expert laughed and said he had just looked over a survey that had shown that the hardest-drinking people around San Francisco were the American Indians in the Oakland slums and the residents of the Tiburon peninsula in Marin County. I didn't laugh quite as heartily as he did, because, although his point was both just and striking, I happen to live on the Tiburon peninsula myself and have for the past seventeen years.

The peninsula, which encompasses the communities of Tiburon and Belvedere, whose combined population is 8,000, is one of the most affluent sections of one of the richest suburban counties in the United States. Marin County as a whole runs neck and neck with such other enclaves of upper-middle-class prosperity as San Mateo County, to the south of San Francisco; Montgomery County, in Maryland; Westchester County, New York; and Los Alamos County, New Mexico. The current "effective buying income" (after taxes) for an average Marin family is between eleven and twelve thousand dollars.

The 200,000 people who live in Marin's 520 square miles have available to them an abundance of the tools of leisure—besides the bottle—that is surely rivaled only by the best situated of retirement communities, which the towns of this county decidedly are not. The residents are on the whole working people—lawyers, architects, doctors, advertising men, vice presidents of something, stockbrokers, sales managers, and so on. Most of them travel daily to San Francisco to earn the means to enjoy what is just possibly the closest any Americans have yet come to the dream of the Good Life.

The evidence is impressive. To take one example, the fortunate people who live on Belvedere lagoon, where houses on narrow lots can be bought for seventy-five thousand dollars and up, can board their Lidos and El Toros from docks in their backyards and sail until a neighbor hails them to come ashore for a drink. For sailors to whom the lagoon is cribbed and confining there are two yacht clubs from which they can sail out into the thirty-knot winds of San Francisco Bay or through the Golden Gate into the great Pacific itself. There are two tennis clubs on the peninsula, with swimming pools and a total of fifteen courts, most of which seem to be in use most of the time except when a winter storm is actually lashing their surfaces. A little farther away are eight golf courses. Ocean beaches are within an hour's drive. Only twenty minutes away is the foot of Mount Tamalpais, with lakes stocked with trout and a network of hikers' trails through the redwoods and madrone. Twenty-five per cent of the county is occupied by park and recreation areas, with the great redwoods of Muir Woods and the rolling moors and white cliffs of Point Reyes offering the most dramatic prospects.

While entertaining friends from Washington, D.C., we drove them one afternoon from our house on the bay through the forests of Mount Tam to our weekend shack on the mesa at Bolinas, which looks out over the Pacific. The trip took barely an hour. Our friends protested smilingly that it was hardly decent to live among such a concentration of good things. I thought I detected a note of puritanism in their envy, a suggestion that, as in the soap operas, true happiness cannot be bought, even in California.

Dramatic! Beautiful! Historic!
—MARIN COUNTY CHAMBER OF COMMERCE

A local historian once startled a gathering of his patriotic compeers by reading a paper that began with the observation that Marin is where the sick Indians used to be sent. As a matter of fact, tubercular Indians from around the bay were cared for in the warm and sunny climate of San Rafael, the county seat, where the penultimate of the Franciscan missions was established in 1817. Later another Indian gave his name to the county. The story goes that, after having been defeated by the whites, the last chief of the Licatuits became a ferryman on the bay, earning the name of El Marinero, the Sailor, which became shortened to Marin, pronounced Mar*in*. (Just yesterday I drove through a community called San Marin, the old ferryman having been canonized through the grace of a real-estate developer.)

Perhaps those sick Indians can perform a useful symbolic function for us. Although much has happened in Marin during the years since then, the county has managed to avoid being drawn into the main currents of California's growth, and even now, in spite of its remarkable rate of population increase, it survives as a sort of refuge, a

By KENNETH LAMOTT

sheltered place. After the Americans came and, by means both fair and foul, divested the original rancheros of their lands, Marin became dairy country, which in its remoter parts it still is. Bypassed by the gold rush, it prospered bucolically. In the latter years of the nineteenth century the theme of the Good Life began to assert itself as well-to-do San Franciscans built summer cottages on its hills. Belvedere acquired a mildly racy reputation for the frolics that went on in the houseboats anchored in its coves. Tiburon became a railhead for the Northwestern Pacific and qualified for its own reputation of raciness by virtue of the inordinate number of saloons that lined its main street. Elsewhere, other towns took on the outlines of personalities they still enjoy: Sausalito, charming and schizophrenic, divided between the solid citizens on the hills and the free spirits on the waterfront; Mill Valley, green and a touch artsy-craftsy; Ross, with its great estates, rich; San Anselmo and San Rafael, rather stuffy.

Over the years the number of commuters has multiplied to the point that driving across the Golden Gate Bridge during the evening rush is an experience that, remembered, can bring on the night sweats. Still, even the bridge has not entirely overcome Marin's isolation. As the other four counties that ring the bay have drawn unto themselves such industries as electronics and aerospace, Marin has remained almost virgin, the purest of bedroom suburbs. Improved industrial property accounts for only 1.5 per cent of the tax assessor's rolls, a statistic of which we homeowners are made painfully aware when our truly horrendous bills arrive each fall. (There is a persistent story that to keep the money rolling in, a deputy county assessor periodically takes to a helicopter to check on newly built swimming pools.) It is clear that one pays for the Good Life.

Why do I play so much tennis? Because I *love* it! —A MARIN LADY

Marin supports more than nine hundred organizations. A recent count came up with 98 parents' groups, 39 women's clubs, 105 church groups, and 30 musical organizations. There are also 216 sports clubs and teams. I don't happen to be an active participant in any of the latter organizations, although, for reasons I don't entirely understand, the two females in my family find it necessary to belong to two different tennis clubs.

On a weekday not long ago I happened to start out for one of these clubs and, having made a false start, ended up stopping at both. At the first club twenty women in pretty white dresses were whaling away at tennis balls. Mostly in their thirties and forties, they were well-tended, tanned, muscular of arm and leg, and intensely involved in their games. While some of them inclined to a pat-ball style of play, there were others who swung their rackets with a fervor that reminded me of one husband's comment that tennis was, at least, cheaper than psychiatry. Changing courts, a couple of the fervent types called hello to me and then went on with their game. *Thwack! Thwam! Smash!* In my mind's ear I heard womanly voices chorusing *Take that*, and *that*, and *that*, and, being the only male in the vicinity except for the club pro, who was stringing a racket in his shop, I retreated.

At the other club some thirty ladies of similar aspect were engaged in the morning's round robin. The club's round robin, which goes on five days a week, is based on an organization of regulars and substitutes that is treated with the seriousness of the order of battle for a major military engagement. Players give up their places on the roster only for the gravest reasons —family bankruptcy, a mortally sick child, or pregnancy. The prudent husband does not treat lightly dinner-table accounts of round-robin politics. Tennis is a serious business. As I approached one court, I was greeted by a lady of mature judgment and quick

intelligence who will willingly play tennis seven days a week, mornings and afternoons. Feeling like a spy from a foreign country, I completed my errand and fled.

Later that morning, needing paper clips or rubber bands, I walked to the dime store in the shopping center. The round robins were over, and the tennis players were now in the shops. Marin is not the sort of place where women go shopping in bathing suits. Even shorts are not looked upon with favor. Tennis dresses, however, enjoy a general dispensation. Perhaps it is their virtuous whiteness; perhaps their association with vigorous and laudable sport. Yet it has struck me forcefully, both on the courts and in the shopping center, that ladies' tennis, at least as we know it on the Tiburon peninsula, is a phenomenon whose psychic depths have never been adequately plumbed.

Fortunately it is not often that a citizen of the United States has the opportunity to witness one group of Americans bent on the deliberate destruction of other Americans through the open and illegal use of firearms . . . Such an incident took place in Marin City, Marin County, California, on the nights of July 27 and 29, 1967. —MARIN COUNTY GRAND JURY

Before attempting a theory of leisure and the Good Life, we are obliged to consider two of Marin's minorities, the most isolated of whom are the Negroes. There is really no place for Negroes in Marin, and their one sociological function often seems to be, as in the grand jury's naïvely shocked report, to remind us of the realities of life in the world outside. (On the nights referred to, fires were set, and firemen and deputy sheriffs were shot at by snipers. Three people, including a little girl, were wounded.)

There are now between four and five thousand Negroes in Marin, or about 2 per cent of the population. Half of them live in Marin City, which started its life as a wartime housing development for shipyard workers and which has now turned into a model of well-designed apartment buildings and houses on a site for which the local real-estate developers would willingly give their collective eyeteeth. Nevertheless, Marin City remains a ghetto, with all the familiar problems of rootless and angry young men and families supported by hard-working women who do the domestic work for their white sisters.

Half the remaining Negroes are prisoners in San Quentin, which for more than a hundred years has occupied a sort of limbo in the county in spite of its formidable yellow walls, and is easily forgotten except when our jurors are called to pass on knifings in the Big Yard or assaults on guards.

Most of the rest of the Negroes in Marin are serving as airmen at Hamilton Air Force Base.

With the exception of an exceedingly small number of professionals, Marin's Negroes have little experience of the Good Life as the rest of the county knows it. Their problems are not the problems of the white people on the lagoons, the bay shores, and the hills. If there is substance to the rumors I have heard occasionally that some of the young men of Marin City have been thinking of making forays, armed with Molotov cocktails and firearms, upon the nearby white towns, then our problems will merge forcibly with theirs in a way whose outcome is hard to predict and dismaying to think about.

> In other counties, a lot of drug use is rather "laudable"—gaining insight, discovering hang-ups, and so on. It's a little less "laudable" in Marin. Here, it's more a pleasure thing. There's nothing else to do.
> —SANFORD J. FEINGLASS

The other, and greater, minority is the kids.

Having three children myself, I have given a good deal of thought to the lives they lead and have arrived at the considered judgment that Marin is a lousy place for kids to grow up in. Like the Negroes, they stand outside the Good Life, which is largely a white adult notion. For the kids, it's great to be able to camp out on the slopes of Mount Tam or dig in Indian burial mounds or play tennis after school seven days out of ten the year round or sail an El Toro out of the back yard, but the real thing that's on their minds is *What's it all about, man?*, and the style of life we've evolved here doesn't give them a very convincing answer.

And so our kids get stoned and drop out of school and make love without prudence and contract gonorrhea and get abortions and sometimes boost cars. Some of them do, at any rate. Others do other things, like becoming eagle scouts and getting into college and going to work or getting killed in Vietnam or getting married and raising families. But it's the other side of the coin that interests me. Somehow, compared with other communities, the kids in Marin seem to accomplish less than they should, and their problems seem proportionately larger.

Their more serious troubles often come pretty close to home. One of my oldest boy's friends—a gentle-natured, unaggressive type—is, as I write, in a psychiatric clinic in San Francisco recovering from a prolonged love affair with an amphetamine called speed. In an attempt to go beyond my own household observations, however, I looked up a couple of experts on the lives the kids really lead.

Sanford Feinglass is an unlikely type to find working as an educator in drug abuses for a school board. A dark, round-faced young man, he turned out to be both articulate and irreverent. We started with the assumption that pot, speed, and acid are available at every school in the county, from junior high up, in spite of the efforts of a sheriff's squad of narcotics agents.

"I came in with fairly clear ideas," Feinglass told me, "but they're getting more and more clouded as I deal with the kids. They've been lied to all their lives. Every time we tell them that marijuana poisons the body, we create thirty disbelievers.

"And so the kid looks at his mother and says, 'Okay, mommy, you use your drug and I'll use mine.' Well, alcohol and marijuana fulfill the same social purposes. Until we can level with them, the kids are going to continue to use."

He went on for a while about the significance of glue-sniffing as an initiatory ritual and then came back to the kids in Marin who use drugs so freely. "There's nothing else to do," he said. "There's nowhere else to turn. Maybe the problem's greater because there's a greater literacy here and more awareness of the failures of society. The kids' great need is the need to get involved and to do something meaningful. The city streets are in some ways a lot better," he added.

In another conversation John Parker, the youthful education officer for the Department of Public Health, added some comments on other areas in which Marin's performance doesn't exactly square with its self-image. The incidence of venereal disease is going up, as it seems to be doing all over. (In 1967, the gonorrhea rate suddenly doubled, from 175.0 cases per 100,000 population to 341.5 cases.) In spite of the pill, the number of illegitimate births is going up, with the greatest concentration among Caucasian girls between seventeen and nineteen years old. Though still comparatively low, the suicide rate doubled between 1962 and 1967.

But statistics tell only part of the story. "We don't really know what the problem is," Parker said, "because our abortion laws are geared to the sort of people we have in Marin County. Poor people have to go to a butcher, but our girls can have relatively safe abortions elsewhere—Tijuana, for instance. Some of the increase in VD may be due to the growing hippie communities in Larkspur and Fairfax, but it really runs through all socioeconomic levels."

> Out in Marin, a man can rest awhile and think of building the Good Life.
> —HERBERT GOLD
> THE SATURDAY EVENING POST

Clearly, we golden people of Marin hardly fit into the classic stereotype of the lotus-eaters, jaded by their pleasures and dying of boredom. We work too hard to support our claims on the Good Life to begin with; besides, we spend too much of our time and energy suffering.

Our troubles, like those of our kids, are often connected with drugs and sex. Our favorite drug is of course alcohol, although as Daniel Meyerson, who is executive director of the Marin Institute (which used to be called the Marin Institute for Alcoholism) put it, "People not being tidy about their symptoms, we get a lot of drugs."

As is the case with alcohol, there is very little of a really original nature that one can do in the way of sexual behavior. There was a brief scandal a few years ago when a quiet weekend wife-swapping circle came to light in one of our least swinging communities. More recently two young and attractive couples of my acquaintance exchanged partners permanently and sorted out the children. They have gone on living in the same town with the same friends, an arrangement that would not, I think, be as readily accepted in the East. In general, however, our troubles with marriage and sex usually end up as simple divorce, though at a rate about twice that on the East Coast. Some time ago I remember reading in the county daily that the divorce rate in Marin had risen above 50 per cent. Among the people I know, it sometimes seems higher.

If alcoholism, drug addiction, and divorce are three indicators of unhappiness, a fourth is those constellations of the symptoms of psychic distress that are lumped together as "mental illness." Figures for mental illness are hard to interpret, and I offer only the contribution that for some years after World War II there was a single psychiatrist in private practice in Marin County; last year the yellow pages of the telephone directory listed forty-three of them, or about one-eighth of Marin's medical community.

And so we are obliged to resolve a paradox. There *is* distress in Eden. The pursuit of the Good Life evidently exacts payment above and beyond the dollar cost of its support. It is easy to fall back on the puritan ethic and suggest that man was not put on this earth in order to enjoy himself, but I would rather not take this way out. Instead, I would like to propose an alternate theory.

Here in Marin we don't really have any more leisure than anybody else does. We do, however, feel differently about it than somebody who lives in, say, New Jersey. The intensity with which we go about our games is the essential clue.

How can anybody possibly be unhappy when he can indulge in his favorite pleasures so easily and so often? The answer, I think, lies in a subtle shift that I seem to see when I travel from West to East and back again. The people I know in the East tend to identify themselves primarily in terms of their professional lives. They are writers, editors, television people, government officials first of all. Here in Marin we are first of all sailors, golfers, tennis players, drinkers, talkers, fathers, philanderers. This is an inexcusable oversimplification, but there is an essential truth in it and one that bears some interesting consequences.

We are talking, of course, about the old question of ends and means. Is a job primarily the means for making possible the Good Life, or is it something worth doing in itself? I don't think I'm being unfair to my neighbors here in Marin—or to Californians generally—when I submit that here, much more than in the East, the job, whether it is a profession like the law or an occupation like selling insurance, is merely the means, and the Good Life is the end.

This change in values affects the sexes quite differently. For the man, the displacement of his center of gravity from his office to his home tends to

OVERLEAF:
Sunday afternoon, Detroit
TONY RAY-JONES

strip him of the great buttress to his masculinity that lies in the mystique of his profession. He becomes, literally, domesticated, and acquires a formidable expertise in coping with the games and toys with which we occupy our leisure. For his wife, there is not even the escape to the office, diluted though this antidote may be. Once her youngest child is in school, she must make the terrible decision as to how she will spend her time—or to put it more directly, how she is going to spend the rest of her life. Judging from the evidence we have seen, the choices are neither sufficient nor satisfying. And so we see these estimable women, the wives of doctors, architects, and lawyers, in tennis dresses and cotton frocks, tanned and well-preserved, wandering the aisles of our supermarkets with a glint of madness in their eyes.

The Good Life can be a busy life, full of activity and then more activity; but why is it that our children stupefy themselves with drugs and disappear into the yeasty precincts of the Haight-Ashbury? Why is it that the young wife of the surgeon has taken an overdose of sleeping pills again? Why is it that so many people one knows have been divorced at least once? Why do we drink as hard as the Indians do in Oakland?

The pathetic and dreadful secret is out: *Nothing really matters very much.* Winning a yacht race is just as important as winning a case in court. Playing a first-rate game of tennis is just as important as painting good pictures. Remodeling a house with one's own hands is just as important as taking a class of freshmen through *Heart of Darkness.* Nothing really matters very much, but the view of the bay is great.

Kenneth Lamott, novelist and disconsolate resident of Marin County, is now at work on a book about California, to be published by Little, Brown.

Is there a
"Lesson of Munich"?

Whatever it is, says our author, it has been
misapplied to Vietnam—just as the "lesson of Vietnam"
may be tragically misapplied in the future

By EDMUND STILLMAN

Nothing could be more naïve than the notion that a fixed record of the past exists. History is infinitely plastic, a panorama of dimly seen events onto which each age projects its own anxieties and concerns: hence we have the repeated phenomenon of "revisionist" historians incessantly reinterpreting the actions and motives of men.

For the rank and file that fought its battles, the American Civil War may well have been a grand quasi-theological drama of the breaking or the preservation of a previously sacrosanct Union. But it was to be reinterpreted three quarters of a century later, in the midst of the Great Depression, as a squalid economic contest of industrial-banking North against agrarian-debtor South, and again by black historians in our own racially obsessed age as a contest between two varieties of white racism—Lincoln's and Robert E. Lee's, honkies all.

Or take the Cold War, which has variously been understood as a desperate defense of an embattled "Free World" against an expanding international Communist conspiracy, as an aggressive effort by America to rob the Soviets of their national security and legitimate World War II gains, as a contest for the allegiance of Afro-

Asia between political systems and "development models," servile or free, and most recently as a mere delusional combat between two ideologically obsessed would-be superpowers whose influence is inevitably fading.

Which cold war is true? Or are all these cold wars true?

Experience is the club with which an elder generation beats the young—but if no one can truly say what happened, and why, in history, the experience of the outgoing elders is less relevant than they may care to think. What may assert itself as the wisdom born of sad experience may only be the elders seeking to redeem the shame or folly of their own youth in wholly distinct or inappropriate circumstances—to the cost of the young.

There is no better case in point than the relevance—or irrelevance—of the lesson of Munich to the war in Vietnam. The men who made this war, or, more accurately, involved America in it, invoked the great historical parable of the appeasers and the aggressors. They never ceased to tell us that they were applying the one certain lesson of the 1930's—that the appetite of the aggressor is always insatiable and to stand against the aggressor early is to avoid a later and vaster grief. In Viet-

nam, the argument goes, there was an identifiable aggressor at work (the "North," Communist China, "Communism") that, at some future time, would threaten the political and physical security of the United States— just as in 1938 Hitler seemed merely to threaten Czechoslovakia but really threatened the freedom of Britain and France.

It is hard to know what to make of this argument—because it cannot plausibly be made in literal terms. The disparity between the relative physical power and potential technology of Hitler's Germany in 1938 and that of North Vietnam (or even of Communist China) today is too grotesque. But even if we suppose that Ho Chi Minh is a petty Hitler whose success must by example whet the appetite of other, greater aggressors, the argument is still in trouble.

For in the prewar world that Hitler menaced there were plenty of petty fascist dictators, just as Ho Chi Minh is a petty Communist dictator in the shadow of greater kindred states. In prewar Europe Hitler and Mussolini were not the only fascists, still less the only aggressors. There were King Carol's Rumania, Admiral Horthy's Hungary, the empty-headed "Colo-

nels'" Poland, the last two thirsting for the flesh of hapless Czechoslovakia as much as Germany. These petty fascist states, and others like them, all contributed to the deterioration of political standards in Europe before World War II. All threatened, in the general sense, the survival of democracy. But they did not, in any practical sense, threaten the physical or spiritual existence of Britain or France; and it cannot be said of Chamberlain or his French coappeaser Daladier that they were derelict in failing to strike at the petty fascisms, when it would have meant dissipating what meager strength they had at that time.

To strike at the petty fascisms of Europe—even the fascism of Francisco Franco that was then advancing to victory in Spain—would have done little to hinder Hitler or Mussolini. For Britain or France to commit their sketchy military strength to irrelevant theatres of diplomacy and war (like the Iberian Peninsula, which was as marginal in that day as Southeast Asia is in ours) could never, in the long run, have prevented Hitler from amassing greater and greater strength in the heart of Europe and striking when the moment suited.

The lesson of Munich must, in retro-spect, seem a curiously specific one—that *this* Hitler, *this* Germany had to be stopped, just as the lesson of the Korean War was that Stalin, lord of a monolithic Communist empire, needed to be stopped. But that all aggressors everywhere, fascist or otherwise, need to be forcibly checked is questionable. The by-now canonical lesson of Munich simply will not bear the weight we put on it; it has already cost us too dearly.

Indeed, if there is any analogy between the 1930's and the Vietnam war, it is not Munich but the Spanish Civil War—a bloody conflict in which surrounding states invested some men and material—and much delusion and emotion—to little ultimate effect.

Spain, like Vietnam, was the *cause célèbre* of its day, enlisting the emotions of the left and right, radicalizing opinion throughout the world. But failing to stop Franco meant very little in the long run. For the Nazi armed forces, Spain was no vital "training ground" for victory. Despite the despairing rhetoric of those years, Spain was no dress rehearsal for a coming Armageddon, no harbinger of a fascist victory, no death knell for freedom. The Spanish tragedy in the end remained what it had been in the be-ginning—a parochial tragedy that settled nothing about the future of Europe. When, soon after Franco's victory in 1939, a greater war began, Spain was all but forgotten.

The trouble, then, is that we are all a little too apocalyptic, a little too historicist in our thinking. No doubt we shall now inappropriately apply the Vietnam experience, failing to intervene sometime in the future when practical wisdom indicates that we should. We are always looking for the Great Lessons of History when there may be none at all—only the smaller lessons: that wisdom lies not in ideological imaginings but in pragmatism; that turmoil and aggression are likely to be with us always, sometimes threatening us and sometimes not; that any nation, however strong, must husband its strength against real challenges from real quarters; that no generation can truly replay history, redeeming ancient follies. And finally, that the elders must not carelessly bleed the young.

Edmund Stillman, a former Foreign Service officer, is the author, with William Pfaff, of Power and Impotence: the Failure of America's Foreign Policy (*Random House, Inc.*).

BERNINI

Behold the roots of Heaven: they are made of stone

By SANCHE DE GRAMONT

If Rome, a city where the monuments of successive civilizations coexist as peacefully as museum exhibits, seems to appear to us today mainly in seventeenth-century garb, the illusion is due largely to the efforts of a single artist. And if St. Peter's, the hub of Catholicism, appears to pilgrims as the symbol of a triumphant, militant church, that too belongs to the vision of Giovanni Lorenzo Bernini.

It is hard to think of Bernini as merely an architect and sculptor, rather than as the director of a vast program of urban renewal, a sort of seventeenth-century Italian Baron Haussmann. Among his contributions to Rome are the church of Sant' Andrea al Quirinale, the angels lining the bridge that crosses the Tiber in front of Castel Sant' Angelo, the two fountains in the Piazza Navona, the Palazzo di Montecitorio, where the Italian parliament sits today, the St. Peter's colonnade, where statues of ninety-six saints and angels stand like sentinels atop pillars of faith, and the great bronze canopy, or baldachino, inside St. Peter's, an example of man-made petrification as startling as a stone leaf. The same man also sculptured the busts of two kings and a score of popes, cardinals, and noble Italians, as well as making their deaths more decorous, thanks to his funerary chapels and tombs.

To explain how Bernini kept undisputed control over artistic life in Rome for more than half a century, thereby

The Piazza of St. Peter's in Rome, above, Bernini's masterpiece, is formed by a keyhole-shaped free-standing colonnade. Acting as silent protectors of the faithful, the massive travertine columns, right, cast deep shadows on the cobbled piazza.

Bernini's Saint Bibiana, c. 1624, is depicted in the joy of martyrdom.

In the Ecstasy of St. Theresa *Bernini used natural light to intensify the drama.*

David, 1623, in mid-action, is the essence of Bernini's dynamic style.

profoundly affecting the style of a great city and a universal church, is to pull together such disparate elements as the artist's life span, the policies of popes, and the Counter Reformation. First, there was the accident of long life. Born in 1598, Bernini lived to the age of eighty-two, serving eight popes. How different Rome would have been had an exceptionally healthy pope commissioned eight successive sculptors!

Bernini was a prodigy. Working in marble at the age of twelve, he already displayed an infallible sense of the human anatomy. He was also unusually fortunate. His father was a minor sculptor of Florentine origin who had come to Rome to work on projects for a Florentine pope, and it was this circumstance that brought the son's talent to the attention of the papal entourage. He acquired a wealthy patron at an early age—the pope's nephew, Cardinal Scipione Borghese.

Bernini appeared just at the moment when the papacy was going through its most intensive phase of art patronage. To commission great works and support famous artists was to enhance the personal luster of a pope's reign. A funerary chapel at St. Peter's was the highest mark of status among the families that competed for the papacy. Great religious art also added to the temporal and spiritual glory of the church. Control over the best-known artists gave the popes the illusion of temporal power after their actual power had begun to decline. And at this critical period of church history artists became missionaries, propagators of the faith at the service of Counter Reformation ideals.

The Council of Trent, ending in 1563, had taken eighteen years to establish a bold front of resistance to the Protestant heresy. Church dogma was redefined and church administration reformed. The ardor of the clergy and the faithful was rekindled by encouraging a siege mentality. There was the church triumphant, the only true church, and on the other side of the moat the heretics who sought to destroy it. This mentality was at the same time militant and defensive.

It trumpeted church doctrine while guarding against impurities that would dilute it. Art was placed at the service of dogma. The Council of Trent ruled that all religious art had to be approved by bishops. It had to be pure, both in style and subject matter. Nudes were proscribed from religious art. Specialists in fig leaves came to be much in demand. Paul IV at first wanted to cover Michelangelo's *Last Judgment* in the Sistine Chapel but finally settled for having Daniele da Volterra paint in a minimum of modesty. Popes Innocent X and XI had the Christ child swaddled. Caravaggio was criticized because his Saint Matthew was barefoot.

By the time Bernini began to accept papal commissions, the Counter Reformation was over its initial puritan phase and had entered a period of artistic exultation, of which he became the most important exponent. He was a truly pious man. He took communion twice a week, went on an annual retreat, and attended mass every morning, like a priest. His favorite book was the *Imitation of Christ*, and a close friend was the General of the Jesuits. Imbued with the spirit of the Counter Reformation, he was naturally drawn to themes that defended what the Protestants attacked: the cult of saints and martyrs, and allegorical figures like angels. All those aspects of the church that repelled Protestant sensibilities became his favorite subjects.

He even managed to put sensuousness at the service of the church. Discerning tourists have long been puzzled by the figure of Saint Theresa in the Cornaro chapel. With her head thrown back as in a swoon, lips parted, eyes half shut, she seems to have been caught in an unguarded moment of sexual fulfillment. Charles De Brosses, an eighteenth-century French magistrate and writer who traveled widely in Italy, commented after seeing the statue of the saint: "If that is divine love, I too have known it." But Bernini was merely being faithful to the Spanish Carmelite's own description of her "transverberation," when her heart was pierced by the fiery arrow of divine love.

Bust of the Spanish jurist Pedro de Foix Montoya was done in 1622.

Portrait of Thomas Baker, 1638, captures the foppery of an English cavalier.

Bust of Urban VIII, c. 1640, one of many done of Bernini's patron.

In Freudian terms the description is an obvious sexual fantasy. "Beside me, on the left hand," wrote Saint Theresa, "appeared an angel in bodily form, such as I am not in the habit of seeing except very rarely . . . in his hands I saw a great golden spear, and at the iron tip there appeared to be a point of fire. This he plunged into my heart several times so that it penetrated to my entrails. When he pulled it out, I felt that he took them with it . . . the pain was so severe that it made me utter several moans. The sweetness caused by this intense pain is so extreme that one cannot possibly wish it to cease."

In the Saint Theresa and in his *Death of the Blessed Ludovica Albertoni*, in the Altieri chapel, Bernini adopted the Counter Reformation belief in ecstasy as an attitude of sainthood. Instead of the naïve, untroubled saints of a Fra Angelico, his are shown with muscles contorted in religious devotion and faces expressing divine love in explicitly physical terms.

A pitiless, unromantic view of death was another Counter Reformation theme. Bernini went to the macabre iconography of the Middle Ages and borrowed the death's head for his tombs. The skeletons holding an hourglass in the tomb of Alexander VII and a scroll in the tomb of Urban VIII proclaim that even such illustrious men cannot triumph over time, and that their judgment is yet to come.

The odd thing is that it was in this restrictive period of church history that Bernini pioneered a sculptural and architectural style much freer than that of the Renaissance. He would have been furious at being called baroque. The word, used originally to designate irregularly shaped pearls, first came to mean any work of art that startled through an extravagant and suspect originality, and later signified a specific art style. But Bernini thought of himself as classical. The authority of the ancients, he said, was unchallengeable. He copied Greek sculpture and was inspired by its themes. He explained that "sometimes, to imitate nature, we must do what is not in nature." It was in this manner that he was able to rationalize distortion as an element of classical style.

Distortion was also a plastic expression of the Counter Reformation mystique: Bernini's subjects are frozen in some moment of action, as though reminding the faithful that the church was engaged in a mortal struggle against dangerous adversaries. Michelangelo's David is an ideal figure, outside time, placid, in repose, a monument of latent strength. Bernini's David is seen at the precise moment when he is firing his sling at Goliath. His muscles are strained, his nostrils flare, his eyes glare under furrowed brows, his mouth is set in determination. In nearly all Bernini's large works, and even in some of the busts, energy is being expended. In its broadest sense, his baroque style is the artistic expression of a restless, anxious society caught between two eras of humanism, having left the Renaissance and not yet reached the Enlightenment.

Because his sculpture is narrative, Bernini experiments with techniques for conveying movement and emotion in stone. He sought sculptural alternatives for the painter's use of shadow and color. In his depiction of the martyrdom of Saint Lawrence marble flames lick up toward the saint. (To get a lifelike expression, it has been said, Bernini scorched his leg with a brazier and sketched the reflection of his own grimaces in a mirror.) In *Pluto and Proserpina* the god is carrying off the terrified maiden, whose flesh yields beneath his grasp. To show grief, Bernini sculptured its visible expression: a marble tear.

All this, as his critics have shown, is a highly theatrical sculpture of overstatement. Bernini had the hand of a sculptor and the instincts of a scenic designer. Not only are the religious figures intended to communicate intense devotion, but the composition of the chapels inside the churches serves as a link for the faithful between heaven and earth. This is particularly striking in the chapel designed for the Cornaro family in the church of Santa Maria della Vittoria. In the center of the chapel there is the white marble group composed of Saint Theresa and the angel. But flanking

the group on either side are marble members of the Cornaro family, sitting in loges like first-nighters, watching rather distractedly the performances of the saint and the angel. Some are chatting, others reading books (missals, one hopes). Light filters over saint and angel from a hidden source. From the earthly involvement of the Cornaros, so like our own, to the painted stucco clouds on the ceiling, Bernini covers the whole religious experience, from life to life after death.

The popes were delighted with Bernini's work. In exchange for subsidies and favors that made him the peer of princes, he flattered them with busts while they lived and immortalized them with chapels after they were dead. He also found admirers in the college of cardinals, source of potential popes. When he had finished the bust of the Spanish jurist Pedro de Foix Montoya, Cardinal Barberini came to admire it and said, "It is Montoya petrified." Montoya wandered in at that moment, and Barberini said, pointing at him, "This is the portrait of Monsignor Montoya," and then, pointing to the bust, "This is Montoya."

In 1623 Cardinal Barberini became Pope Urban VIII and, according to a probably apocryphal anecdote, told Bernini: "It is your great good luck, *Cavaliere*, to see Maffeo Barberini pope. But we are even luckier in that the *Cavaliere* Bernini lives in the time of our pontificate." Bernini was put in charge of the papacy's entire artistic program, and until Urban's death in 1644, he was almost wholly occupied by papal commissions. The pope insisted on monopolizing his output, with one or two exceptions—King Charles I of England and Cardinal Richelieu were given Bernini busts done from portraits in exchange for political favors. A wealthy Englishman named Thomas Baker paid him the equivalent of ten thousand dollars for a bust. The pope scolded him for undertaking so plebeian a project, so Bernini had the bust finished by an assistant. But his friendship with the pope was hardly of the tempestuous sort that had existed between Michelangelo and Julius II. Bernini had free access to the papal apartments, and the two often spent the evening there together until the pontiff dozed off, the signal that Bernini could leave after adjusting the window blinds.

Responsible for multiple projects, Bernini became more a contractor than a sculptor. He had the power of a high

The high altar, right, of St. Peter's, Bernini's most spectacular achievement, is crowned by the Cathedra, or Throne, of Saint Peter. The twisted bronze columns, also by Bernini, support the baldachino, or canopy, over the saint's tomb. At left is pictured the throne, haloed by a glory of Bernini angels.

LEONARD VON MATT—RAPHO-GUILLUMETTE; BELOW: ALINARI

curial official. Other artists complained that he had a stranglehold on patronage, and critics charged that he was bankrupting the papacy. When he plundered the bronze portico and the roof of the Pantheon to make his baldachino, it was said that what the barbarians could not accomplish had been done by the Barberini. He employed a growing number of sculptors and stonemasons to carry out his designs. To be an artist in Rome, it was said, was to work for Bernini. When he was not designing, he worked on his busts, chiseling the marble for hours without stopping. Short and thin, with the profile of one of the pope's falcons, he had the energy of a long-distance runner, the passion of one of his own marble saints, and the efficiency of a seventeenth-century organization man.

Pope Urban took a fatherly interest in his gifted protégé. When Bernini fell ill, the pope visited him twice a day in his *palazzo* near the Piazza di Spagna and once came with sixteen cardinals, whose collective blessing was intended to spur a prompt recovery. During his visits the pope urged Bernini to marry; he had an investment to protect from the temptations that ravage the flesh. In 1639 the dutiful Bernini married the young daughter of a lawyer, who bore him eleven children. Another worry for the pope was the tempting offers that came from abroad. Cardinal Mazarin tried to lure Bernini to France with the promise of a salary raise. "Projects in France are begun in heat but end in nothing," the pope warned.

The death of Urban in 1644 was a double blow for the *Cavaliere*. Because the pope had raided the Vatican treasury to finance his embellishments of Rome, large-scale patronage was interrupted. There was a city resolution directed against Bernini as "the instigator of the popes' indulging in useless expenses in such disastrous times."

Furthermore, Urban's successor, Innocent X, was an enemy of the Barberini family, and Bernini fell into a disgrace compounded by an architectural error: a bell tower he had built on the façade of St. Peter's caused cracks in the structure of the church and had to be removed. Bernini's rival Francesco Borromini, who had started out doing minor tasks for the *Cavaliere*, came into favor. But disgrace gave Bernini opportunity for private commissions, and it was during this time that he designed what he considered his

Pluto and Proserpina, *right, a rendering in marble of violent action, was done by Bernini at age twenty-four. As the detail shows, Bernini strove to convey what was at the time an utterly novel sense of immediacy in sculpture. Movement sweeps back Proserpina's hair and drapery, while Pluto's fingers press in her seemingly yielding flesh.*

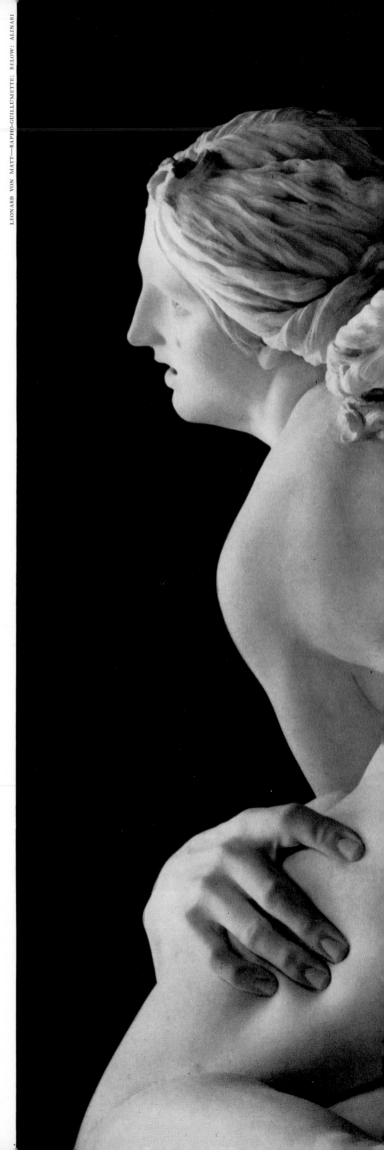

BOTH: LEONARD VON MATT—RAPHO-GUILLUMETTE

most accomplished work: the chapel for Cardinal Cornaro.

Innocent X soon caught the virus for building. He erected a large family palace on the Piazza Navona, flanked by Borromini's twin-towered church of Sant' Agnese. When an impressive Egyptian obelisk was discovered in the Campagna, the pope decided it would be just the thing to decorate a giant fountain that would set off the church and the palace and make the Piazza Navona the artistic triumph of his pontificate. Bernini did a model of the proposed fountain, which a friend judiciously left in a room where Innocent X was bound to see it. Once again Bernini was summoned to the Vatican.

In his fountain design Bernini returned to the Counter Reformation theme of the church triumphant, spreading through four continents, which were represented by personifications of four rivers—the Danube, supporting the papal coat of arms and accompanied by a lion; the Nile, with its head covered by a cloth (because its source had remained so long undiscovered); the Ganges, with an oar (because so much of it is navigable); and the Río de la Plata, with coins representing the wealth of the Americas. The pope was pleased with the gushing rivers in their tropical décor of palm trees and fronds, but Bernini in later life came to hate the fountain and would have the shutters of his carriage closed when he passed it.

It was thanks to Bernini that the next pope, Alexander VII, went down in history as the *papa di grande edificazione* (the "pope of great buildings"). Under his pontificate Bernini designed the most important architectural creation of the Roman seventeenth century, the colonnade of St. Peter's. Bernini considered architecture a sideline, although he boasted that sculptors made the best architects, because they were students of the human body and the classical orders (Doric and Ionic) were based on human proportions. He went to work designing an enclosure to pen in the crowds that came for papal benedictions, the visitors to the city (*urbs*), who represented the rest of the world (*orbis*). His two free-standing colonnades embraced the faithful in a pincerlike movement, at once welcoming and protecting them. For most if not all Catholics the physical center of

The Blessed Lodovica Albertoni, above, a Roman widow who gave all her wealth to the poor, was portrayed by Bernini in the throes of death. The detail at left shows the artist's superb, emotion-rousing depiction of her blanched face and dying gaze.

Bernini's bust of Louis XIV is regarded as the "grandest" of baroque portraits.

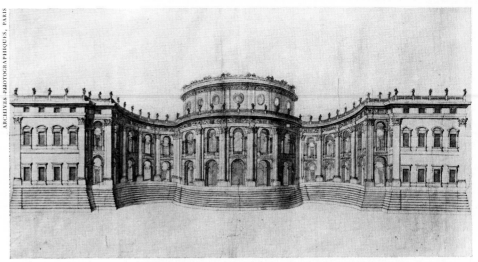

The first of Bernini's four plans for the east façade of the Louvre, done in 1664, was so unlike anything seen in France that it caused a scandal at the court of Louis XIV.

the church, more than Jerusalem or Nazareth, is this great keyhole where the Vicar of Christ resides.

Work on the colonnade was interrupted in 1665 by a summons from Louis XIV and the *Cavaliere's* first and last visit to a foreign court. The Sun King, then only twenty-seven, had already initiated a building program suitable to his fame. He wanted Bernini to design the eastern façade of the Louvre. At the same time, the invitation was part of the monarch's policy to diminish papal prestige. Already in 1662 the Duc de Créqui, French ambassador to the papal court, had shamed the pope by forcing him to dismiss his guard and threatening French occupation of the papal enclave at Avignon. To pluck the world's most famous living artist from the most important task of his career was another affront to Alexander VII. Though delicately phrased, the king's invitation was not of the sort that could be just as delicately turned down. Bernini could not even plead his age, which was sixty-six.

Bernini spent nearly six months at the French court, but except for a marble bust of the king, which had been commissioned as an afterthought, the trip was a failure. It was a foregone conclusion that an artist who believed his gifts came from God and who had been employed all his life by God's vicars on earth would clash with a king who considered himself crowned by God. Two forms of divine right collided, as did also two chauvinisms.

At their first meeting Bernini traded compliments with Louis XIV. He said he would outdo himself for a king of such superb taste. "Let me hear of nothing that is small," he said. The king replied that Bernini was the cleverest man in Europe. But Bernini was unable to keep up the niceties for long. After visiting the Tuileries with the king, he told Louis through an interpreter, "*che li pareva una grande picciola cosa*" (that it seemed to him a great tiny thing). He frowned at nearly all that Paris had to offer. The pleasant jumble of rooftops reminded him of a carding comb. He told Jean Baptiste Colbert, Louis's first minister, who was also Superintendent of Buildings, that the Val de Grace cupola was

like a little cap on a large head. When he visited the tomb of François I and his family, he said: "*stanno qui molto male*" ("they must be very uncomfortable here"). Colbert's face clouded. Mansart, Bernini advised, might have been a great architect had he studied in Rome; while French painters, with their thin, sad manner, should visit Lombardy and study Raphael. Only Poussin found Bernini's favor. Colbert said he was glad Bernini had finally found something he liked.

Nor could Bernini adjust to customs of the French court. He was used to taking a nap after lunch, a time French courtiers reserved for visits. He was careless about etiquette, and courtiers mocked him for calling the Comte d'Harcourt *Excellence* instead of *Altesse*.

Particularly annoying to him was the habit idle courtiers had of dropping in while he was working on the king's bust. Dozens came and went each day to watch him perform. The progress of the bust was a major event. The length of the king's nose, the heaviness of his jaw, and the tilt of his head were discussed with the same urgency as the success of French armies on the Flanders front.

Bernini had ordered three blocks of marble, complaining when he received them that they were "*cotto*" ("brittle"). He then sketched the king as he went about his daily occupations, playing tennis, at cabinet meetings, and on one occasion as the royal foot was being bled. "Movements reveal all the personal qualities which are his and his alone," Bernini explained. Once when Louis XIV looked over his shoulder, Bernini said, "*sto rubando*" ("I am stealing"), and the king replied in Italian, "*si, ma e per restituire*" ("yes, but you will give it back").

Meanwhile the same courtiers who had at first treated Bernini as an infallible artistic authority, asking for his advice on everything from a staircase to a tomb, now began to spread rumors about his presumptuous behavior. They said Bernini was a miser who undertipped his servants. They repeated alleged remarks made by him while he was working on the king's bust: "*Questo è bello; nell'originale, questo*

Bernini's terra-cotta model for his equestrian statue of Louis XIV portrays the monarch as a classical hero.

The monumental statue was changed to represent Marcus Curtius by order of King Louis, who detested it.

vero è bruto" ("What I am making is beautiful, but the original is really ugly"). They said that after visiting the king's private apartments in the Louvre, Bernini had said, "*non ci sono qui stanze per uomini*" ("these are not rooms for men"). Louis XIV cooled toward Bernini after hearing the rumors. He said with regal understatement: "It is true that he does not praise much."

After forty days the bust was finished. It is a monument to absolutism rather than a faithful likeness. Bernini smoothed the bump on the Bourbon nose and enlarged the king's small eyes. He tried to wrest from the marble the same effects that the king's portraitists achieved with color. He modeled a flat curl on the royal forehead and chiseled shadows around the eyes. (He regretted not being able to duplicate the king's long lashes.) Bernini was pleased with the result and told an admirer that what Michelangelo had once said also applied to him: "*Nelle mie opere caco sangue*" ("In my works I shed blood").

Meanwhile, Bernini's Louvre design, a huge façade with his trade-mark of the concave-convex flow, detached columns on the outer and courtyard fronts, and a cornice crowned by a balustrade, was running into interference. Bernini complained that Colbert was obsessed by minutiae. There was little common ground between the visionary Italian and the practical Frenchman. Bernini wanted to express grandeur in stone, while Colbert badgered him with details about plumbing and sewerage. To be asked such things, Bernini lamented, was like the king granting audiences to paupers and widows begging for pennies.

The storm broke during a work session with Charles Perrault, one of Colbert's assistants. Perrault told Bernini that his design did not leave enough room for the kitchens. Bernini penciled in a few changes. Perrault complained that he had a notebook full of unanswered queries about Bernini's work. He said that he and many others wanted to know why the west façade would be lower than the east. Bernini, whose temper was at the breaking point, explained it was for reasons of general harmony. And in any case, he blustered, when it came to craftsmanship, he would accept criticism only from someone more capable than himself, not from someone like Perrault, who was not worthy to clean the soles of his shoes. "A man like me, to be treated thus," shouted Bernini. "I'll complain to the king—I am leaving tomorrow, and I don't know what keeps me from taking a hammer to my bust after so much contempt has been shown me."

Bernini left Paris without thanking either Colbert or the king. France had not suited him. He did not travel well. His art was linked to the physical and intellectual climate of Rome and the papacy.

Shortly after Bernini's brusque departure the Louvre façade design was awarded to Claude Perrault, the architect brother of the courtier who had goaded Bernini into losing his temper. Perrault's design was sober, elegant, and traditionally French in its motifs. It was ample evidence that the artistic formalism sponsored by the French court could not have assimilated the lushness and extravagance of a Bernini in any large-scale project.

Bernini's trip was a double failure. Not only was the sculptor unable to impose his artistic views upon the French, but at the same time the center of artistic patronage passed from Rome to Paris. The papacy had lived beyond its means too long. It could no longer dazzle Europe with its panoply of artists. This role was now assumed by Louis XIV; for in France, too, patronage of the arts was one of the expressions of power. French national style became increasingly exclusive. Bernini had promised to make an equestrian statue of Louis XIV. It did not reach Paris until 1685, five years after the sculptor's death. Louis took such a strong dislike to the bare-chested, bareback horseman that he ordered the statue broken. Relenting, he had it touched up by one of his academic hacks, renamed *Marcus Curtius*, and banished to a remote corner of the Versailles park, where it still stands. Back in Rome's more hospitable *ambiance* Bernini finished his interrupted work on the colonnade. Also, as a tribute to Alexander VII, he designed the oddly comic monument that stands in front of the church of Santa Maria sopra Minerva:

an Egyptian monolith growing out of a baby elephant's back. It has the startling quality of some of the more celebrated surrealistic juxtapositions, such as the umbrella on the operating table. But as the involved conceits on the inscriptions show, the monument was not intended to be bizarre. It was the emblematic glorification of the papal reign. A jungle beast and a pagan obelisk became the paradoxical symbols of an elderly pope's wisdom and holiness.

Bernini lived on to serve three more popes, but they made fewer demands on his talent. His declining years were matched by a decline of papal influence in the European balance of power, and a resulting scarcity in commissions. When his right arm became paralyzed, Bernini jested that it was a well-earned rest for a member so long overworked. He died a few days before his eighty-second birthday, in the midst of his designs and assistants while working on the restoration of the Palazzo della Cancelleria.

Charles Perrault left an acidulous description of Bernini: "His mind was quick and brilliant, and he had a great gift for inspiring admiration. He was a great talker, full of rhetoric, parables, and anecdotes, with which he seasoned all his conversations. He praised and approved only the men of his own land. He quoted Michelangelo about everything, saying *Si come diceva il Michelangelo Buonarotti* ['as Michelangelo used to say']. He said he had a great enemy in Paris, 'the opinion that they have of me.' "

Bernini could not have complained about the opinion of Romans, for he had earned their gratitude. The inscription on the house where he lived reads: "Here lived and died Gian Lorenzo Bernini, before whom popes, princes and the people bowed reverently." Less reverently, Romans today are fond of saying that Bernini died at eighty-two after falling into the baroque.

Sanche de Gramont has written about spies and covered the Vietcong; he may be the only Frenchman ever to win a Pulitzer prize. His most recent book is a history of the ancien régime in France, Epitaph for Kings (*G. P. Putnam's*).

In the Piazza Navona, above, stand Bernini's "Fountain of the Moor," foreground, and his mighty "Fountain of the Four Rivers." The detail at left shows the personification of the Ganges.

CLIMATE
AND HISTORY

What turned the Sahara from
the fertile land of prehistoric paintings (above)
into a rocky desert (below)?
What caused the collapse of great empires in
the twelfth century B.C.?
What brought desolation to Greece in the
seventh century A.D.?

On the evidence of history
and meteorology, a distinguished classical scholar
proposes a clue to the rise and
fall of civilizations in the eastern Mediterranean

No one doubts that the climate of the earth has undergone important changes in the past. The series of ice ages that have come and gone is sufficient proof of this. But such long-term fluctuations were ascribed to remote geologic time, until recent investigation brought a different perspective and it became certain that the last ice age had ended only a few thousand years ago—twelve thousand, to be specific. By 7000 B.C. Europe and North America had become as ice-free as they are today. But it is not correct to assume that once the great ice sheets over the continents melted away, the whole earth's climate grew steadily warmer, as though a huge planetary refrigerator were being defrosted. On the contrary, pollen analysis of the peat bogs of northern Europe has revealed that some seven thousand years ago the region must have enjoyed a climate considerably warmer than that of more recent time; and during the subsequent millenniums there have been several recurrences of decidedly colder conditions. Marked alterations in climatic states thus belong not merely to geologic aeons but to actual human experience in the past, and we know of at least two regressions in civilization that may be directly ascribed to climatic change.

While the ice sheet was still spread over northern Europe, extending south almost as far as London and Paris, the glaciers and snow fields of Switzerland still farther south, being larger than at present, threw a formidable barrier across the southern part of the continent. Between these two impassable fronts—the solid ice to the north and the snow-blocked mountains to the south—a corridor of open country led west from inner Asia to the Atlantic coast. At the end of this corridor, in what today is France, where the winds brought moisture from the unfrozen Atlantic and somewhat tempered the rigors of the atmosphere, there lived a race of hunters amid the herds of wild animals—reindeer and bison and mammoth—on which they fed. All that we know about this rude and hardy folk has been learned by exploring the caves in which they took shelter and in which they left us the bones of the animals that they ate, some of the tools that they made from such bones, and, remarkable beyond all, the superb colored drawings of the animals that they hunted.*

One might suppose that as the icecap receded, existence would have become easier for these ancient hunters. But the new warmth and the increased moisture altered the steppelike grazing grounds of the animals on which the hunters depended for food and raiment. Scrub growth gave way to forest; swamps and marshland replaced the open pastures. In search of the old way of life to which they were accustomed, the animals (and after them the hunters) seem to have wandered away, under the climatic shelter of the retreating icecap, through the great European corridor across Russia into Siberia, where we lose sight of them. Those of the hunters who stayed behind had to adapt themselves to new and less bountiful conditions, snaring and trapping and fishing. Compared with the abundant life of the great game-hunting days, this was an impoverished sort of existence, since the secrets of plowing and sowing and animal breeding were as yet unknown. Artistic skill disappeared; craftsmanship diminished; all life had to be lived on a meaner level of subsistence. This was the first great cultural recession of which we have certain evidence and of which we can confidently say that it was caused primarily by a climatic change.

The next occurrence was surprisingly different, and to those who have never examined the evidence, hardly credible. It centers on the formation of the great North African desert known to us as the Sahara, which is as large as the whole of continental Europe. Improbable as it may seem, the melting of the icecap over northern Europe at the close of the last ice age occasioned the transformation of vast stretches of flourishing pasture land in North Africa, far away from the ice, into a waterless and barely habitable waste. As the ice retreated in northern Europe, the desert expanded in Africa.

How was this possible?

The prime cause of this astonishing transformation was the ever-blowing trade wind, for the trade wind creates and maintains the desert zones that girdle the continental regions of our planet in the northern and southern tropics. Where this

*See "The Lascaux Puzzle," page 94.

persistent rush of air crosses the oceans it leaves no recognizable mark of its passing, but where it streams overland it leaves aridity in its wake through a zone as much as a thousand miles wide. At the two confines of the wasteland that it creates, the trade wind begins and again ceases abruptly, as though coming from nowhere and journeying nowhere. But here there is no mystery, for it begins its course by descending from far aloft and ends it by rising skyward again, leaving beneath it the equatorial calm of the doldrums. The mechanism of this seemingly unmotivated behavior is well understood. The heating power of the overhead equatorial sun creates as it were a vast chimney of upward-climbing warm wet air. On reaching the colder upper atmosphere this air sheds most of its moisture through condensation, to produce the rainfall of the equatorial regions. But the air itself, drained of most of its water, cannot descend against the unceasing upward draft and so is forced to drift away over the roof of the world, northward and southward toward the poles. However, it cannot complete its poleward journey because it encounters the so-called polar front in the temperate latitudes, which blocks its progress and forces it to descend. As it does so, it becomes steadily warmer (and therewith drier) under the increasing pressure of the atmosphere until, on nearing the earth's surface, it divides into a pole current that starts the cyclonic rainstorms of the temperate zones spinning and a great draft of air that returns toward the equator. It is this unceasing return draft that constitutes the trade wind. Growing steadily warmer as it moves through lower latitudes, it will pick up moisture, thus desiccating the lands over which it blows and causing all but the hardiest of vegetation to wither. Since the belt of the trade wind is roughly a thousand miles wide, we should not be surprised that this is the average extent of the Sahara from north to south.

This great circulatory atmospheric system is not tied to the geographic equatorial line but to the position of the sun relative to the earth; so that as the sun moves north and south in the sky during the year, the trade-wind belt in either hemisphere will move responsively, although with much

lesser range. In the northern hemisphere, and specifically in the eastern Mediterranean, during late July and August the belt of the trade wind shifts north with the summer sun until its regime of rainless weather covers the Aegean. Thus during the summer of every year the climate of the Sahara prevails over most of Hellas.

During the ice age climatic conditions in the Mediterranean basin must have been very markedly different from those of later time. V. Gordon Childe stated the situation briefly and vividly in *The Most Ancient East*:

While Northern Europe was covered in ice as far as the Harz, and the Alps and the Pyrenees were capped with glaciers, the Arctic high pressure deflected southwards the Atlantic rainstorms. The cyclones that today traverse Central Europe then passed over the Mediterranean Basin and the Northern Sahara and continued, undrained by Lebanon, across Mesopotamia and Arabia to Persia and India. The parched Sahara enjoyed a regular rainfall, and farther east the showers were not only more bountiful than today but were distributed over the whole year, instead of being restricted to winter . . . We should expect in North Africa, Arabia, Persia and the Indus Valley parklands and savannahs, such as flourish today north of the Mediterranean.

In brief, during an ice age there should not have been any desert where the Sahara is today, and geologists, zoologists, and ethnologists all agree that this was indeed the case. The geologists say that rivers were running full stream, carving out the gorges and stream beds whose dry courses may be seen today. The zoologists say that tropical varieties of fish and aquatic animals such as crocodiles and hippopotamuses made their way up these now dried-up rivers, to live and reproduce themselves in what is now the very heart of the desert. The ethnologists report that on the rocks that were once the walls of water-filled gorges there are engraved drawings of giraffes and elephants, crocodiles and leopards, and other animals such as do not exist, and could not survive, in the present environment. When the great ice sheet retreated over northern Europe, the polar front moved back with it, and the zone of the trade wind expanded, thereby creating the desert that exists today.

Meanwhile to the east beyond the Red Sea a similar event was taking place in Arabia, where, along the same latitude and from the same natural cause, a second and smaller area was likewise turning to desert and forcing its inhabitants to migrate. Here then were two great reservoirs of well-established humanity that could no longer offer food and water for more than a small fraction of their erstwhile population. From the desert of Arabia came forth the Semites; from the desert of North Africa were dispersed the Hamites, moving in all available directions to occupy new lands. This great exodus from the Sahara and central Arabia is the second discoverable instance of a momentous impact of climatic change.

Herewith, it is generally assumed, the epochal examples of man's response to climatic upheaval came to an end, since nothing comparable in magnitude to the passing of an ice age has happened since. Such a view is entirely wrong. To quote a leading historian of climate: "The present day does not differ from the past; variations of climate are still in progress, similar in kind, though not in extent, to the climatic vicissitudes of the ice-age."

This being so, we are entitled to shift attention from geologic to historic time and to inquire whether there are adequate grounds for postulating that the trade wind that today brings drought to Saharan North Africa has at any times during the comparatively recent past extended its parching effect farther north, to assail Greece with aridity.

The primary proposition is extremely simple: if in the past the size of the north European icecap has directly influenced the size of the North African desert (in the sense that this desert zone has widened as the ice retreated northward), this process should continue on a small scale as well as on a large one and hence should still be operative whenever the glaciated portions of our planet expand or decrease. During the past ten thousand years, after the bulk of ice age glaciation had melted in Europe, there have demonstrably been periods of considerably greater warmth than at present, alternating with periods of returning cold. The crucial question is whether this has been happening on a large enough scale to produce any climatic alteration capable of affecting human history. One may be inclined to object that, since these fluctuations probably did not involve an increase or decrease of more than 2° or 3° or possibly 4° Fahrenheit in the overall daily average temperature of our planet, they might have discommoded or gratified our remote ancestors, but hardly forced them to change their habits or their habitations. But to raise this objection is to misunderstand the possible effect of even small increases in planetary temperature on the specific area in which we are here interested. For the primary issue is not the state of mean annual temperature in the Aegean or elsewhere, but the behavior of the trade wind and the course of the temperate storm tracks during periods of diminished planetary glaciation.

Each summer, as we have seen, what we might term the earth's heat equator is displaced northward, so that the operation of the trade wind shifts—although by no means consistently. Whereas the sun moves through some 23½° of latitude, the trade wind following the summer sun shifts through approximately no more than 10°; but this is equivalent to a northward displacement of nearly seven hundred miles. In Attica and on the Cyclades there are so few showers between late May and September that the year's vegetation withers and dies and the skies grow hazy and dull. By adapting themselves to these conditions nature and man survive successfully; but were the rainless zone to spread farther and endure longer each year, the resulting effect on human and animal ecology might assume extremely serious proportions.

Specifically, if the trade-wind zone were to move farther north, following the retreating polar front and a general rise in planetary temperature, the storm tracks along which rain is presently conveyed eastward across the European continent would suffer displacement toward the north, thereby leaving the Mediterranean subject to the prevailing westerly winds, whose orographic condensation of moisture evaporated from the sea would accrue only to the western slopes of the mountainous lands in their path, leaving the interior tracts of land consistently dry during most months of the year.

It is now pertinent to inquire whether

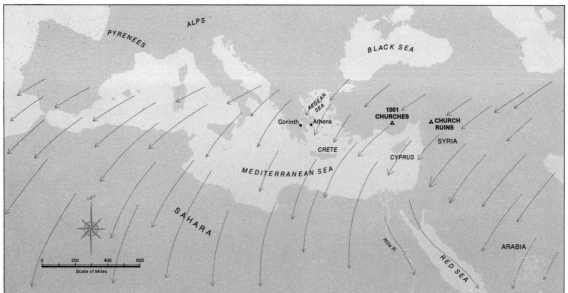

The trade winds, which bring no rain, sweep over the Sahara throughout the entire year and create its desert climate. The map above shows the present course of the trade winds in midsummer, when they have their farthest northward movement and temporarily carry the Sahara climate to the Aegean area. In other centuries, our author believes, the winds moved farther north, bringing disaster to civilizations in their path.

professional investigators of climatic change postulate the occurrence during historic time of warm phases sufficiently pronounced to induce the phenomenon just described, and if so, whether the approximate dates that they assign to these phases synchronize with any retrogression in civilization that written history or archaeology establishes for the Mediterranean world.

To deal with this latter evidence first, leaving the meteorological evidence for later examination, it may be asserted with entire confidence that in the course of the past three millenniums there are discoverable at least two instances of catastrophic decline in human well-being and cultural attainment centered on the eastern Mediterranean. These took place at intervals of about eighteen hundred years.

The second of these cultural retrogressions in the Mediterranean deserves much more extensive treatment than it has received from historians. If it is discussed at all, its terrible toll of human misfortune is generally ascribed to disastrous contemporary events of a political or politico-economic kind. But in most histories of the Mediterranean the seventh century A.D is largely a blank; and of this blank in cultural history I have myself had some experience while digging on the site of ancient Corinth.

There the American excavators have more than once dug down through the unimportant Turkish level beneath the present surface and encountered a flourishing layer of Byzantine occupation attributable to the eleventh and twelfth centuries A.D. Below this, if a second and older Byzantine level is met before the period of late Roman imperial rule is reached, that level will invariably belong to the fifth and sixth centuries. Except for an occasional stray coin, the seventh and eighth centuries are missing. What went wrong in the seventh century that it should have left no trace? Some historians would say that the gap is due to the invasion of Greece by half-civilized Slavic hordes. But these do not seem ever to have reached Corinth; and on closer examination the Slavic conquest turns out to have been chiefly a sporadic unwarlike penetration by nomad shepherd bands moving in with their families, animals, and household goods, not so much conquering as refilling an empty land. A Byzantine chronicler confirms this by remarking that "Greece was Slavicized after the plague had depopulated the world." Plague there was, certainly, and starvation; but these are calamities that may have climatic cause. Other historians maintain that it was the Arab pirates who pillaged and thus depopulated seventh-century Greece. But the country

can be proved to have been just as empty in regions where the Saracens never set foot.

Elsewhere in the eastern Mediterranean there are signs of similar catastrophes. In the heart of Turkey there is a region called today "the thousand and one churches," with the same exaggeration that has bestowed on the famous collection of Arab stories the inaccurate title of *The Thousand and One Nights.* But while there never were a thousand churches there, the number of them built during the fifth and sixth centuries of our era testifies to a very sizable population. But during and after the seventh century no more churches were built, and those already in existence were allowed to go to ruin. Today they stand empty and desolate. Who killed off their congregations? The Arabs and after them the Seljuk Turks, say the historians; but the chances are better than even that here again the historians are wrong. The real problem seems to have been the failure of the local water supply due to a lack of adequate rainfall over a long period.

Farther to the East, in Syria, there is an even more spectacular assembly of early Christian stone churches, testifying to an extensive population during the fourth and fifth centuries but likewise implying abandonment and collapse during and after the

Proof that the level of the Mediterranean has varied can be seen at Pozzuoli, near Naples, where this Roman temple has been inundated. The drawing above shows how ancient ships were moored. The rings still exist but are now seven feet below water level.

seventh century. What caused the catastrophe? The Moslems of the Arab conquest, say the political historians. Yet the Arab subjection does not seem to have been so bloodthirsty. "Not a single Syrian town was captured by force of arms," says a recent student of the period; "all accepted the easy and generous terms of the Arab chieftains: Jew, Samaritan, and Christian alike welcomed the Arabs as their deliverers from Greek oppression." What, then, caused desolation amid the stone churches? It was the drying up of the springs through failure in the annual rain supply, without which neither man nor beast nor growing vegetation can survive.

Even while the Mediterranean was suffering the setback that I have illustrated for Greece and Turkey and Syria, northern Europe was prospering. In England, we read, grapes could be ripened and wine made—a feat impossible in Roman times. In Ireland the monasteries reached a height of prosperity and learning unequaled until then. In Scandinavia the population had increased to the overflow, colonization level by the ninth century. During the following decades there began the great stream of Norse emigration to Iceland and to Greenland beyond.

The name Greenland is apt to strike us as a rather grim joke, but at the time of its settlement the coast was green enough with vegetation to merit such a name. Not until the late thirteenth century did polar ice close in on the lower Greenland coast. By the end of the fourteenth century conditions had become so unfavorable that the white men had to retire from the land, to be replaced by Eskimos from the Arctic. But now in our own time the northern ice cover has been melting back in a spectacular (though perhaps only temporary) retreat, revealing the cemeteries of the old Norse colonists.

Thus we find that the bad centuries in the Mediterranean have been good centuries farther north, while the inclement centuries in the north have been favorable to man in the south. For it was just when the northern seas began to freeze over again after A.D. 1000, during the stormy phase from the twelfth to the fourteenth centuries, that civilization in and about the Mediterranean resumed the great upswing that carried it through the Renaissance into modern times.

This, then, may be the great climatic cycle by which the career of European civilization has been controlled.

I now turn back to much earlier times, to the centers of civilization before the emergence of classical Greece. The calendar time is 1200 B.C., and Mediterranean man has begun to suffer the most severe cultural recession that history records or archaeology can determine. Great kingdoms have collapsed without apparent adequate reason; and the eastern seashores are overrun with fugitives seeking to force their way into lands less smitten by disaster. In Greece the well-fortified Mycenaean palaces are burned and abandoned, but no one seems to know who burned them. In the heart of the Anatolian plateau the dynasty of Hittite kings, who had treated on equal terms with the Pharaohs of Egypt, abruptly comes to an end. Their capital city is abandoned.

What has happened? Nobody offers any valid explanation. The Egyptian records of a few years earlier speak of a severe famine in the Hittite land and of shipments of grain sent in aid by the Pharaoh. And some recently published correspondence between Hatti and Syrian Ugarit speaks of a shipment of two thousand measures of grain to be conveyed in an Ugarit ship as "a matter of life or death: let the king of Ugarit not linger!"

In Greece the wealth and splendor of the Mycenaean Age vanished utterly, to be succeeded by those miserable centuries of hand-to-mouth existence of which Thucydides seems to have had some hearsay knowledge when he wrote that, long before his day, Greece had been "without commerce, without communication by land or sea, cultivating no more acreage than the necessities of life demanded, destitute of capital, building no large towns nor attaining any form of greatness." To which vivid picture we may add that Greece had become illiterate (even as the old Egyptian priest was reported to have told Solon in Plato's *Timaeus*). There is no surer indication of cultural collapse than the failure to transmit the use of letters, once this use has been acquired.

What had happened?

Historians have made their usual suggestions—foreign invaders, barbarian hordes overwhelming the eastern Mediterranean; in Mycenaean Greece the Dorians, driving down from the Albanian highlands; in Asia Minor the Phrygians, crossing from the Balkan highlands. But archaeology does not bear out these explanations. Like the Slavs in the Middle Ages, when the climatic cycle had run full circle, the Dorian Greeks seem to have moved into a depopulated land, bringing their wives and children and goods and chattels in a haphazard and unwarlike migration. And in Asia Minor the Hittites seem to have deserted their ancestral sites and moved southeast through the mountains into northern Syria centuries before the Phrygians ferried themselves across the Bosporus and took possession. South of the central plateau "the coasts were restless," according to a contemporary Egyptian record; "no land withstood them . . . they came with fire before them, onward against Egypt." They were met and repulsed by the alarmed Pharaoh in what he boasted was a tremendous victory. But what set this motley crowd in motion? No one knows—unless it was hunger that drove them; for they came not as lone raiders but with their wives and children, by ship and by oxcart.

So it was, from one end of the Mediterranean to the other. Even Egypt, which had resisted the attack of the shorelanders, lost its vigor and sank into a helpless apathy that was to last for a full four hundred years.

No competent historian today doubts the seriousness of this major recession of civilization, a recession that spread throughout the Mediterranean lands at the close of the thirteenth century and lasted, with only occasional and very local remission, until the ninth century B.C. It was a widespread collapse of prosperity and power almost unparalleled in any other place or period in the civilized career of man. Yet no one has so far been able to offer any adequate explanation for its occurrence.

To my thinking, after puzzling for many years over this, the greatest still-unsolved problem in Mediterranean history, there is only one solution that will meet all the varied aspects of the case, and that solution is—*famine*, a dropping of the food supply below the critical level for subsistence. And by famine I do not mean an occasional failure of several consecutive harvests, but such an enduring and disastrous destruction of the annual yield as only a drastic climatic change could have occasioned.

But what proof have we that such a climatic change actually overwhelmed the Mediterranean lands about 1200 B.C. and lasted through several centuries until, around 850 B.C., a climate returned that was more favorable to human existence? How can we tell what climatic conditions prevailed in a past so far removed and seemingly so inaccessible to examination?

One piece of evidence is the variation in the level of water in the seas, caused by the freezing and thawing of the polar icecaps. Scientists have reached the conclusion that at the height of the last ice age so much of the planetary water was heaped over the land in a frozen state that the general ocean level sank some three hundred feet! Looking in the other direction they now calculate that if all the polar ice were to melt away, enough water would be released to raise the planetary water level more than two hundred feet higher than the present shoreline.

Now, the geologists and the physicists may run into insurmountable difficulties in trying to determine the exact planetary water level for any given date in the past, but it is possible that the archaeologist can help them out. By fixing his attention on man's occupation of the Mediterranean shoreland during the last three to four thousand years, the archaeologist may be able to discover where the water level stood and thus infer what the overall climatic conditions were for many of the crucial periods of human history.

In Italy at Pozzuoli, near the mouth of the Bay of Naples, there are remains of the old Roman harbor works that marked that port as the leading maritime station in the Mediterranean. These remains include brick and concrete buttresses that once supported an arcading for a dock or breakwater. On some of these the metal rings for fastening ships' hawsers are still in place, but they are seven feet below the present water level. Since no one ties ships to underwater rings, but to moorings at least three or four feet above the water, it seems that at the time when these rings were put in place (probably close to A.D. 140) the level of the Mediterranean was some ten feet lower than it is today. But some of these same piers have been attacked by marine borers, such as are still to be found in the Bay of Naples, and the pittings and perforations made by these shellfish, which never emerge from the sea, extend up the piers for almost ten feet into the air. Hence it would seem that at some period between Roman times and our own the level of the Mediterranean has been ten feet higher than it is now. Thus in this one spot there is a record of fluctuation of twenty feet in the earth's ocean level in the past eighteen hundred years.

Evidence of a rise of the sea since the classical period exists along the Sicilian and North African shores in the western basin of the Mediterranean; and in the eastern basin evidence may be found at Greek mainland sites, at some of the Aegean islands, and along the southern coast of Turkey. In the eastern basin of the Mediterranean at the site of Kenchreai, the ancient Aegean harbor for Corinth, recent American excavations have revealed constructions from imperial Roman times that are at present under six to ten feet of water.

While it is thus a comparatively simple matter to show from the discrepancy in sea level that a colder (and therefore wetter?) climate prevailed in the Mediterranean during the classical period, it is much more difficult to adduce evidence that the contrary condition of increased warmth accompanied by scantier rainfall dominated the preceding late Mycenaean period. There is a considerable body of evidence indicative of such a climatic phase at the end of Roman imperial times; but for the earlier period of the late second millennium before Christ, the traces of high water in the Mediterranean have been obliterated or are no longer legible. Lacking such evidence, we must look for another way to explain the sharp decline in the Mycenaean culture during the thirteenth century B.C. and the virtual extinction of that culture thereafter.

The theory to which the majority of present-day scholars are most partial is the so-called Dorian invasion, to which they attribute the entire calamity of the destruction of Mycenaean sites and the wane of Mycenaean prosperity and power. Their argument runs that some sort of violently hostile invasion could alone have been responsible for so much irreparable damage, and since Greek historical tradition records no other newcomers into Greece between Mycenaean and classical times, *ergo* it is the Dorians who must have destroyed the Mycenaean realm.

Before demonstrating the outright impossibility of making the Dorians responsible for the collapse of Mycenaean civilization, it is essential to provide some sort of reliable picture of material conditions in southern Greece toward the close of the Mycenaean Age. Such a picture is supplied by Vincent Desborough in his authoritative work *The Last Mycenaeans and Their Successors*. Here is his account:

The history of the last quarter of the thirteenth century can possibly be reconstructed as follows. The first sign of trouble is visible in an attack on Mycenae itself; it does not seem that the attackers penetrated within the citadel; but considerable damage was done to imposing buildings immediately adjoining. There is no proof that other sites suffered destruction at this time, nor do we know the cause of the attack. The shock must have been considerable, but was not catastrophic.

Fairly soon afterwards, however, a really serious invasion [of the Peloponnese] took place, the effects of which are visible in destruction of sites, in their desertion, and in a movement of population. Many sites were abandoned without our knowing whether there was destruction as well.

Here I might comment that a better way to put this would be to say that these sites were deserted without any trace of destruction or conflagration! Among the abandoned settlements were:

two important sites in the Argolid as well as some minor settlements, and probably a considerable number of sites in Laconia and the southwest Peloponnese. As a result of this de-

struction and desertion there was a movement of population to less dangerous [why less dangerous?] and, in some cases, originally less populous sites. Achaea in the northwest Peloponnese and the island of Kephallenia are examples of areas where a considerable increase of population is to be observed. The east coast of Attica now becomes more fashionable than previously, and it is fairly clear that a sizeable body of refugees made their way to Cyprus and to Tarsus in Cilicia.

Where did the "invaders" come from? With admirable reasoning, Desborough proceeds to show that the attack could not have been organized from within Mycenaean territory. It must therefore have penetrated from outside Greece. But, as Desborough proceeds to argue, there was no racial group to organize such an invasion and no available route by which invaders might have come, since all the possible routes of entry seem blocked, according to the archaeological evidence, which shows Mycenaean culture surviving in the very regions through which the invaders would have had to pass. In the first place, if the invaders came by sea, says Desborough,

it does not seem possible that they came from the eastern Mediterranean, as they would have had to pass through the South Aegean, which remained unharmed. Also, it is hardly likely that they came down the Adriatic or from South Italy or Sicily, since there would not then have been a movement of refugees to Kephallenia, in the precise direction from which the invaders would have come.

For similar reasons a sea-borne invasion from the northeast Aegean is ruled out, so that the only logical conclusion must be that the invasion did not come by sea.

Desborough continues:

The hypothesis of a land invasion has two merits . . . However, it raises the problem of the invaders' eventual settlement . . . They might of course have occupied all the areas through which they passed, but there are good reasons for rejecting this idea . . . First, it must be stressed that there is no single object or custom which can be associated with the invaders in any region passed through by them.

Secondly, there is evidence of considerable depopulation in Laconia and Messenia, and

in the great majority of cases archaeological excavation or survey shows that the abandonment of sites . . . was an absolute one. That is to say, there was no further occupation of the sites by anyone—at least not until considerably later. This is not a matter of a few sites only; the num-

ber that has now been identified is very considerable. Not only have we no evidence of any alien objects, we have no evidence of any settlement at all. The natural and logical answer is that the invaders did not settle in any of the areas which they overran, but departed.

I submit that a better inference would be that there were no invaders.

What actually happened in late Mycenaean history was not an invasion from outside, but an evacuation from within, not an enemy incursion, but a dispersal of the Mycenaean inhabitants of the Peloponnese. I have already remarked their arrival on the western shoreland of Achaea and the western slopes of the Panachaeic mountains, as well as their migration to Kephallenia (and perhaps to others of the Ionian island group off the western coast of Greece).

By the turn of the millennium at 1000 B.C., Mycenaean civilization had virtually ceased to exist. Yet there was no discernible classical civilization either. Between the two there is a gap of emptiness too wide for any bridge that one might try to build from the pre-Hellenic to the Hellenic world.

About the only source of light we have for this otherwise totally obscure period is the ancient tradition of the Heraclidae. Modern historians have used this legend to support their theory of a Dorian invasion, but ancient writers called it the "Return of the Heraclidae" to their ancestral land. The Greek word for this return was that universally used for an exile's return to the land he was forced to leave— κάθοδος.

At the start of the story the Heraclidae (which is to say, professed linear descendants or tribal followers of the legendary hero-god Herakles) had presumably been inhabiting Argos; but however we identify them, ancient tradition emphatically asserted that they departed from the Peloponnese and betook themselves by way of Attica to northern Greece, whence after a considerable lapse of time their descendants made their way back into the Peloponnese. They brought with them a mixed company of Doric-speaking people, with whom they had become associated during their term of absence from their motherland.

There is no evidence that the return of the

A Viking grave (above) and the ruins of what was once a rich farm (right) are evidence that Greenland at one time enjoyed a much milder climate than it does today.

Heraclidae to their ancestral land in company with the Doric tribes was anything more violent than an unopposed occupation of a depopulated countryside. It is true that Pausanias preserves a tradition that the descendants of King Nestor of Pylos were driven from their home by the Heraclidae and sought refuge in Athens; but Pausanias adds, immediately after, that "there was no expulsion of the ancient Messenians by the Dorians," but a sharing of the land with them under a Heraclid as king. Most of the Mycenaean settlements that were abandoned in the twelfth century were not chosen for reoccupation by the Dorians. The intervening lapse of three generations and a full hundred years of time had obliterated old memories and the physical traces of previous human existence. These changes of abode, which archaeological reconnaissance has established on unarguable evidence, constitute a material proof of historical discontinuity between the two cultural epochs.

Here it might be well to pause and review the situation. Briefly stated, I have been seeking to establish two quite simple propositions: namely, that the Dorians had nothing whatever to do with the collapse of Mycenaean civilization, since they did not enter the Peloponnese until long after that collapse had already taken place; and secondly, that the political and cultural disintegration of the Mycenaean Age was not due to destruction at the violent hands of outsiders, but was engendered from within by local conditions that compelled the abandonment of most of the smaller communities and instigated a sacking of the palaces of the ruling caste, with the result that a hitherto prosperous countryside was left virtually unoccupied, to remain at the lowest endurable subsistence level for the better part of two centuries.

It remains only to inquire whether the facts of meteorology will support these propositions. It seems reasonably safe to say that any rise in planetary temperature, such as occurs from time to time (even though we have no satisfactory explanation of its cause), should produce a weakening of the high-pressure polar front with a consequent further extension of the operation of the trade wind northward into the temperate zone. Since the temperature gradient poleward from the equator would diminish, the intensity of the trade wind might be lessened; but since the trade wind blows all year round, it would still bring drought to the Aegean in summer, while in late spring and autumn it would, by virtue of its more northerly zone of passage, divert the cyclonic rainstorms away from the Mediterranean track along which they now travel. The result for southern Greece would be nearly eight months of well-nigh continuous drought every year instead of the four or five that now prevail.

Whereas cyclonic storms with their veer-

ing vortexes overpass the mountain barriers in their path and are thus able to penetrate the continental interior of Europe and western Asia with their moisture-laden air, westerly winds blowing over the Atlantic and entering the Mediterranean through its western gap have a different action. After picking up moisture from the sea, they tend to discharge it again, in the form of rain, on striking any relatively high transverse mountain barrier. Having shed part of their moisture load on westward-facing slopes, they pass without further discharge across the lower-lying country behind the mountain barrier.

Let us apply these observations to Mediterranean conditions as we might imagine them in a climatic phase of dominant westerly winds. Consultation of a structural map of the Balkan Peninsula will show that the western shoreland of Greece from northern Messenia to Epirus should catch and condense the moisture-laden winds from the Ionian Sea, even while southern Messenia, Laconia, and Argolis would be almost totally deprived of rain. (Remember that the archaeological evidence indicates the abandonment of these interior and east-coast regions in late Mycenaean times and at the same period an increased inhabitation of western Achaea.) The island of Kephallenia, with its seaward exposure and its high central mountain, would be a rain catch.

Beyond the Greek mainland the westerly

55

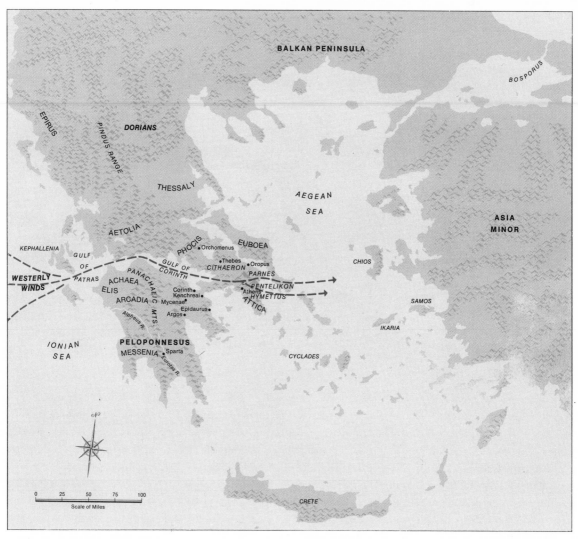

The Aegean world, our author believes, was devastated by drought around 1200 B.C.; but even so, Athens and its vicinity would have continued to prosper. The moisture-laden westerly winds, funneled and cooled by the mountains around the Gulf of Corinth, as the map above indicates, would have brought rain to Attica.

winds, moving across the broad Aegean, would regain much of their moisture (though hardly in time to benefit the nearby Cyclades), bringing rain to the lofty islands of Chios, Ikaria, and Samos, close to the Asia Minor coast, and watering the less elevated continental shore by condensing moisture on the interior upland girdle of heights and ridges to feed the uniformly westward-running rivers. In this view the Ionian migration from the Greek to the Asiatic mainland may be understood as nothing more mysterious than a flight from a drought-ridden to a better-watered land.

But the interior plateau of Asia Minor beyond the rain shed of the broken Phrygian upland would have fared no better for rain than did the Peloponnese—or perhaps even more poorly, because the high mountain walls shutting it off on either hand, north and south, would have contributed toward turning the heart of Asia Minor

into desert wasteland. So it was that the Hittites were forced to move out.

The preceding sketch of climatic conditions in late Mycenaean and immediately subsequent times is in exact agreement with the archaeological evidence for the movements and density distribution of the human population in Greece and the Aegean, except for one seemingly serious flaw. That flaw is Attica. Being the easternmost canton of mainland Greece, Attica, most of all, should have been (one might object) subjected to the effects of drought. Yet tradition maintains that it was continuously inhabited from Mycenaean into classic times, and we have no reason to challenge this.

On closer inspection this apparently fatal objection to my thesis of climatic calamity at the end of the Mycenaean Age turns out to be its most striking confirmation. For the hundred-mile Gulf of Corinth, extending east from its gaping mouth in the Gulf

of Patras, is so shut in on either side by high mountains that it acts as a gigantic funnel for westerly winds. These pick up moisture from the surface of the sea as they pass over it, and this warm wet air is then channeled through the Aigosthena gap beneath Mount Cithaeron and is condensed into rain as it is forced up into the cooling heights of Parnes, Pentelikon, and Hymettus. Thus, granted a regime of prevailing westerlies, while the rest of eastern Greece was dry, the interior of Attica, the *mesogaia*, would be blessed with rain.

Thucydides' claim that Attica escaped conquest by the Dorians because the land was not worth taking, so thin and infertile was its soil, rings singularly false. It not only disagrees with present-day conditions, but it runs counter to Plato's assertion in the *Critias* that the country bordered on the north by Cithaeron and Parnes and the district around Oropus "is superior to all

The onset of a colder climate might explain the difference between the topless garb of Minoan women (above) and the woolen tunics of classical Greece.

LOUVRE—GIRAUDON; LEFT: JOSEPHINE POWELL—HERAKLEION MUSEUM

ERIC LESSING—MAGNUM

HIRMER FOTOARCHIV MUNCHEN

This sixteenth-century B.C. Minoan palace at Knossos was built with a flat roof (top), suggesting a dry climate. Greek temples of the classical period (above) had pitched roofs that were suitable for a rainier climate.

other land in fertility . . . in proof of which, this region is a match for any other soil in its range of fine harvests and its pasturage for all sorts of animals." And no reader of Aristophanes can have missed his praise of the ease of Attic country life with its rich farms and orchards and vineyards. The simple truth is this: the Attic land was never occupied by the Dorians because it was never abandoned by its proper inhabitants, who had abundant reasons for continuing to dwell in it.

This, then, is my interpretation of the archaeological evidence coupled with ancient oral tradition: a "time of trouble" was occasioned by climatic causes that brought persistent drought with its attendant famine to most of mainland Greece, and it was this unlivable condition of their native abode that forced the Mycenaeans to emigrate, ending their century-long prosperity.

There is pretty sound circumstantial evidence that throughout southern Europe and the Mediterranean there was a shift to a colder and wetter climate during the ninth century B.C., culminating at about the middle of the first millennium B.C. Effects of this change include the shift in costume from the seminude Minoan and Mycenaean attire to the heavier classical raiment and, in architecture, from flat to pitched gable roofs, indicative of heavy rainfall. By the time of the first Olympiad, in 776 B.C., from which the classical world dated its historical career, a climatic change had restored fertility to continental Greece.

If we can place any reliance on the suggestion made by several of our climatologists that there is a recurrent climatic swing conforming to a period of about 1,850 years, then by calculating forward and backward from the ninth century B.C. we should encounter a cold and stormy phase at about the year A.D. 1000 and an earlier one at about 2700 B.C. Perhaps it is a mere coincidence—but if so, it is a very striking one—that the later of the two dates, the opening of the eleventh Christian century, coincides quite closely with the ending of the Dark Ages in Europe, as well as with the resurgence of Byzantine power in the Near East; while the earlier date, 2700 B.C., is one that is now pretty confidently upheld for the emergence of enlightened civilization in Egypt under Zoser, the first of the great pyramid builders, and synchronously in Sumer under the First Dynasty of Ur.

If, for the contrary swing of the climatic pendulum toward drought, we take the year 1200 B.C. as our point of departure and count 1,850 years forward and back therefrom, we should encounter a disastrous drought phase in the eastern Mediterra-nean around 3000 B.C. (as to which we are at present ill-informed, but in which there is some slight reason to believe) and another in the seventh century of our era (about which it has been possible to speculate with much greater assurance).

In thus interpreting the phenomena of cultural discontinuity in the Near East, I am reminded of Shelley's marvelous lines:

Life like a dome of many-coloured glass
Stains the white radiance of eternity.

Historians, too, when they view the distant past, dissolve its white light into a set of rainbow colors as they peer through their glasses of political, economic, geographic and geophysical, or anthropological interpretation. Only when the broken colors are reblended will the white light of historic actuality shine forth. In this article I have been looking through some very restrictive lenses, but I submit that the perhaps unfamiliar hue that they have cast over Mycenaean and medieval Greece is no merely random coloring, but a physically actual component of the clear light of truth.

Rhys Carpenter, Emeritus Professor of Classical Archaeology at Bryn Mawr, is the author of Discontinuity in Greek Civilization, from which this article was excerpted by permission of Cambridge University Press.

GHOST DANCE AND CARGO CULT

In times of stress look for the prophets
of an earthly paradise: Handsome Lake or Mohammed,
Lenin or the Teacher of Righteousness.
America may be ready for its own millennial cult

*This self-portrait of a Taos Indian of the
Peyote cult was done about fifty years ago.*

By PETER FARB

Most of the great economic, social, political, and religious upheavals in history—early Christianity, Mohammedanism, the Protestant Reformation, the Russian and Chinese Communist revolutions, the Mau Mau in Kenya, and many others —started out as small cults predicting the imminence of a millennium that would decisively overthrow the established order. When we think about them, these cults are unusual for several reasons. First of all, they are "religious" and evangelical, even though some, such as the Russian Revolution, denied the existence of religion, and others, such as the revolution preached by Martin Luther, opposed the established religion. Secondly, a close study of their histories tells us they combined two things we usually regard as incompatible: earthly material rewards and religious fervor.

The pattern of these historic upheavals is being followed by the numerous prophets, cults, and millenarian movements that have sharply increased in the United States in recent years. Impoverished Americans refuse any longer to be deprived of their share of the nation's material wealth—yet their protests often take a religious form. The Poor People's Campaign, for example, built a "Resurrection City" in Washington, D.C. Store-front salvationists are thriving in northern ghettos. The militant Black Power prophets, although avowedly opposed to established religions, exhibit all the qualities of millenarian cultists; and so do the Black Muslims, who in protest against economic deprivation reach outside America's Judaic-Christian tradition to an alien religion. Maharishi Mahesh Yogi shows his converts the transcendental path to wealth and happiness. Cybernetics preaches a new cult of the machine and the incalculable benefits that will flow to those with faith in a computer age. Marshall McLuhan preaches a new technology and urges us to prepare ourselves for the imminent millennium through communications. Even the traditional religions are becoming deeply committed to economic goals, as churchmen like Father Groppi of Milwaukee spend more and more time obtaining for their congregations secular rewards such as increased incomes, equal job opportunity, and better housing.

Clearly, the present surge of millenarian cults is telling us something important. To understand what it is, we first must disabuse ourselves of two false notions—that they are something new and that they are occurring solely in the United States. Such movements have been seen in every race on every continent, though the better-known ones have occurred among the Indians of North America, the blacks of Africa, and the natives of Melanesia and Polynesia. Nor are they anything new: they have been documented at least as far back as Hebrew times.

Probably more is known about millenarian movements among American Indians than among any other people. Almost as soon as white culture became dominant in North America, prophet after prophet arose. As early as 1762 a Delaware Indian preached a new doctrine that he said had been revealed to him in a vision. The Master of Life told him that the Indians must give up liquor and polygamy and other vices: "Let them drink but one draught, or two at most, in one day. Let them have but one wife, and discontinue running after other people's wives and daughters. Let them not fight one another." If they also performed certain sacred rituals revealed to the Delaware prophet in a dream, they could defeat the British—and be rewarded by both liberation and economic well-being. The prophet's teachings inspired an Ottawa Indian warrior named Pontiac to unite several Indian groups around the Great Lakes. In 1763 his followers attacked the English forts, toppling one after another, including even the fort at Detroit, before the British beat them back and he himself was slain in an ambush.

A millenarian movement that was completely different—because it preached peace and also because it succeeded—arose a few decades later among the Iroquois. A Seneca sachem known as Handsome Lake had become a miserable drunkard; his own personality problems were a reflection of the troubles that afflicted the entire Iroquois culture. The Iroquois, once regarded as "the Greeks of America," had fallen far in only two generations. They had watched their villages burned and looted, their people killed and the survivors dispersed to Canada. Their lands had been taken from them, and they were pushed onto lonely reservations, islands of discontent surrounded by white prosperity. They were defeated and in despair; acute alcoholism was rampant, and the surviving Iroquois quarreled among themselves.

The culture was in crisis when, in 1799, Handsome Lake lay dying of some strange malady. Heavenly messengers came to him and told him the wishes of the Great Spirit: the Iroquois must cease drinking, quarreling, and practicing witchcraft. Although Handsome Lake reported subsequent visions that told of new rituals for the faithful to perform, his attention was really directed toward the economic and social problems of reservation life. He told the Iroquois to switch to the white man's methods of agriculture to increase productivity, and he introduced the plow and cattle among them. He emphasized the farm household and convinced males that they should work in the fields, a task formerly regarded as woman's work. He forbade the Iroquois to sell any more land to covetous whites.

The Code of Handsome Lake, which Thomas Jefferson called "positive and effective," became a blueprint for Iroquois survival in a new technological world and in a new social world of reservation life. As a result, the Iroquois became widely respected by whites for their sobriety and the accomplishments of the new economic pattern of family farming. Handsome Lake's religion—which grafts Quaker teachings onto traditional beliefs about the Great Spirit—is to this day followed by hundreds of Iroquois on reservations in New York and Ontario.

The American Indian millenarian movement that won the most adherents in the last century, though, was the Ghost Dance of the Plains Indians. After the Civil War, as prairie schooners and railroads brought settlers to their traditional hunting lands, the Plains Indians suddenly encountered the full force of manifest destiny. Bison, their food base, were systematically shot until very nearly extinct, in order to starve the tribes into submission. The Indians were rounded up and herded onto wasteland reservations. The American policy was the cultural, social, and possibly even biological extermination of the Plains Indians. The disease, alcoholism, malnutrition, and crowding might have been bearable had not their one possible hope—their traditional religions—been taken away from them.

At the very time when things appeared bleakest for the Plains Indians, they heard about a distant shaman (or medicine man) named Wovoka, a Paiute of Nevada. During an eclipse of the sun in 1889, when Wovoka lay ill with fever, he had a vision during which he was taken to the other world and given a message from God. He was told that the time was near when all Indians, living and dead, would be reunited on a revitalized earth, where they would live without misery or want. Part of the ritual centered around the wearing of a "ghost shirt," a white garment fancifully decorated with symbols of birds, the sun, stars, and arrows. And the return of the dead ancestors could be hastened by dancing. Wovoka also told his people that God said they must "love one another, have no quarreling, and live in peace with the whites; that they must work, and not lie or steal . . ."

The Ghost Dance, as this cult came to be called, was not something suddenly thought up by Wovoka. In the Great Basin the belief had existed, probably long before the arrival of whites, that the dead would return and that this return could be encouraged by dancing. A Ghost Dance movement twenty years earlier had predicted the return of the dead and the destruction of whites in a cataclysm. As Wovoka's peaceful teachings spread, they became confused with this earlier, more violent dance. The Plains tribes heard about Wovoka and sent delegations to talk to him. Ironically enough, these delegations, which would spark the last major rebellion against the whites, traveled on the white man's railroad to spread the news of the Ghost Dance, and they told about it in English, their only common tongue. The delegates reported back on Wovoka's teachings in a very garbled form. They told the Plains tribes that dancing would bring back not only their ancestors bearing gifts but also the great herds of bison, and that the whites would be wiped off the face of the earth by a landslide that would miraculously leave all their possessions behind. Best of all, the Plains Indians would be invulnerable to white attacks because the ghost shirts were supposed to be bulletproof.

The Shoshonis and the Arapaho began dancing at once, and several other Plains tribes soon followed. The Ghost Dance attacked in a particularly virulent way the Sioux, the largest of the Plains tribes. As punishment for their intransigence, in 1890 they were being systematically starved into submission by the cutting off of their rations, on their wasteland reservations in the Dakotas. Present among the Sioux was the spark to ignite a conflagration: Sitting Bull, a white-hating leader and a veteran of the 1876 massacre of Custer's cavalry. The white authorities became alarmed about the spread of the Ghost Dance, and they alerted the army to put an end to the movement. Sitting Bull was killed in a moment of confusion while he was being arrested. Two weeks later, at Wounded Knee, South Dakota, three hundred of his followers, mostly women and children, were massacred by trigger-happy U.S. cavalrymen. Wounded Knee marked the end of the hopes of the Plains tribes and of the Ghost Dance movement itself, although it lingered on until the 1930's. Its promise had inflamed the Plains Indians, but like a prairie fire, the movement burned itself out quickly.

These three American Indian movements, and the hundreds of others that have been documented from all parts of the world, present a single pattern. A prophet emerges from obscurity, as did Jesus, or Mohammed the camel driver, or Wovoka, who never left Walker Lake, Nevada. The prophet predicts a complete upheaval of the economic and social order and the imminence of the millennium; the Jewish Zealots at Masada, for example, thought that Isaiah's prophecies were about to be fulfilled, and Marshall McLuhan tells us that we are already in the new technological age that is making our traditional ways obsolete. Dead ancestors (as in the case of the Ghost Dance) or other liberators (American Negroes in many African cults

From Polynesia to Africa, the cult followers identify with the Jews of the Bible. Some believe they belong to a lost tribe of Israel.

and the American President in some Melanesian millenarian movements) are about to bring relief and the possessions the people so earnestly desire. But the people must prepare quickly for this event by performing rituals (such as baptizing, by the Essenes, or learning the thoughts of Chairman Mao). A new code of morality and law is drawn up (the Code of Handsome Lake or the nonviolent teachings of Martin Luther King), and usually new insignia are adopted (the ghost shirt among the Plains Indians or circumcision among the Mohammedans). And, finally, the faithful must show their loyalty to the new movement (by dancing in the case of the Ghost Dance, by political confession in the early years of the Russian Revolution, by reciting special prayers in the case of evangelical Christian sects, or by feeding the computers with facts in the case of cybernetics).

The pattern of millenarian movements was already well established in ancient Jewish times. The prophetic book of *Baruch* predicts that a Messiah will come to break the power of the Roman Empire and that he will establish a kingdom on earth; pain, hunger, and war will no longer be known, and the earth will yield its fruits ten-thousandfold. Jesus' description of the kingdom of God was interpreted literally by the early Christians as meaning material rewards that will be enjoyed here on earth. Even such church fathers as Papias and Irenaeus expected the earth to bring forth unheard-of bounty without the necessity for cultivation, and the heathens to become the slaves of the faithful. The imminence of the millennium remained a strong belief as long as the Christian church was an unpopular minority. But as its influence increased in the Mediterranean world and it finally won acceptance by Rome itself, the church stamped out millenarian beliefs and dis-

credited the leaders as "false prophets" and "heretics."

Despite attempts to suppress them, millenarian movements continued to occur within the church. The official crusades launched between the eleventh and fourteenth centuries under the auspices of the various popes are well known—but largely unknown are the unofficial crusades of the poor people. Recurrent waves of excitement swept Europe, during which the poor and the hungry followed some miracle-working prophet to the Holy Land. None of these foolhardy and desperate expeditions ever reached its goal, but rather all perished in hostile lands or on dangerous seas. The crusades of the poor people made no distinction between the spiritual Jerusalem and the material blessings the poor expected to find in the earthly Jerusalem. There was considerable rivalry between the papal crusades and the poor people's crusades. In fact the unofficial crusades claimed that they would be successful in capturing Jerusalem and that the knights would fail—because the very poverty of the poor people made them God's elect.

As Christianity spread around the world it prompted millenarian movements both by disrupting native religions and by offering the messianic pattern as seen in the Bible itself. Most of these movements, and *all* of them in places like Polynesia, identified most closely with the persecuted Jews of the Bible. The oppressed found in the Jews a counterpart to their own plight, and many even claimed direct descent from the tribes of Israel. For example, the Hau-Hau movement among the Maoris, the Polynesians of New Zealand, developed when the natives renounced their half-hearted conversion to Christianity and revolted against the British. Their new religion was based largely on the Old Testament. The Maoris believed they were the survivors of one of the lost tribes of Israel led into bondage by the Assyrians; they declared New Zealand to be the new Promised Land, from which the British would soon be ejected, thus ushering in the millennium. When that happened, the Jews would travel from the Near East to unite with their long-lost Maori cousins. In 1865 the Maori rebels captured a British ship and imprisoned all the crew except for one Captain Levy, who, being Jewish, was set free. Thereafter any Jews who reached Maori lands were given haven, although all other whites were killed. The Maoris fought the British with the same fanaticism the Jews had once shown against the Romans. And they were similarly defeated, although the movement lingered on until 1892, when the last outbreak occurred.

The Israelite movement has also been strong in South Africa. About 1910 a native prophet rejected the New Testament as a hoax perpetrated by the missionaries, preaching instead a return to the teachings of the Old Testament: his followers celebrated the Jewish Sabbath and the Jewish feasts, did not eat pork, and regarded themselves as the chosen people of Jehovah. When the South African government attempted to disperse the sect and raze its home village, the fanatical Israelites fought the troops with spears. Revulsion at the massacre of about one hundred and twenty villagers eventually forced the government to recognize the native Israelite churches, and they are well established today in South Africa.

Africans have also found appeal in one of the most successful millenarian movements in existence today. The Watch Tower movement, better known in the United States as Jehovah's Witnesses, was founded in 1872 by a white preacher in Pittsburgh, and it now has a membership of more than a million people in two hundred countries. Its journals are published in European languages and also in Africa in such Bantu languages as Lozi, Shona, Sotho, Bemba, Nyanja, and Zulu. About 1925 a Nyasa native introduced the Kitawala (a mispronunciation of Watch Tower) cult among the miners in Katanga Province in the Belgian Congo. The Africans found the teachings of the Watch Tower much more palatable than traditional Christianity. The Watch Tower preaches the imminent coming of the millennium, when justice will finally reign for all on earth. It denies such Christian tenets as the divinity of Jesus, the Trinity, eternal damnation, and immortality of the soul. It condemns both the state and organized Christianity as instruments

of the Devil. The Kitawala prophet absorbed these teachings and spread them through central and southern Africa, publicly accusing the missionaries of distorting the Bible. He was accused by the white authorities of having killed "baptized people" (a euphemism for "white Christians"), and he was ignominiously hanged from the gallows. Such repression resulted only in the movement's spread with greater vigor into the French, British, and Belgian colonies in Africa.

How are we to explain such seemingly diverse movements as those of the Jewish Zealots and the early Christians, the Maoris of New Zealand, the Kitawala of the Congo, the Ghost Dancers of the North American plains? The earliest attempt to do so was made by James Mooney, who had studied the Ghost Dance firsthand and who is an important source for our knowledge of the American Indian movements; he attributed them simply to "religious abnormalisms." Such an explanation is no more satisfactory than another that became widespread a little later: millenarian movements are an outlet for the superfluous energy liberated by the introduction of modern tools. Other scholars have erected theories that ascribe the movements to mental indigestion caused by the introduction of Christianity to intellects not yet ripe for it—and also to emotional stresses that predispose a people to yearn for deliverance.

Elements of truth can probably be found in each of these explanations, but a much more satisfactory one exists. "The deprivation theory" was first documented about 1935 by an anthropologist, Philleo Nash. His method was to re-evaluate the influence of the first Ghost Dance, that of 1870, on three different groups of Indians—the Klamaths, the Modocs, and the Paviotsos —who had been brought together by the white authorities on the Klamath reservation in eastern Oregon. Each group was made up of several bands, and all of them had the same opportunity to succumb to the hopes of the first Ghost Dance when it reached the reservation in 1871. Yet some bands rejected it, others took to it enthusiastically for a short time and then abandoned it, and still others continued faithful

to its teachings long after it had died out.

Nash delved deeply into the history of each band, and he concluded that it was not simply a case of a band adopting the Ghost Dance if it had suffered great deprivation because of white conquest. More important was whether the band felt deprived of material benefits it had been led to anticipate. He learned that a band of Klamaths—the only Indians who had not fought the whites and who had peacefully accepted white values—participated enthusiastically in the movement. The reason was that the Klamaths had been deprived in their expectations: they had been given white skills that they had no way to use; they had been shown the benefits of white civilization but had not been taught the skills to acquire these benefits. The only Indians on the reservation who had beyond doubt benefited by their identification with whites, and who accepted their values, were the Indian employees. They took no part in the movement—and they even attempted to suppress it.

The deprivation theory is most clearly illustrated by the cargo cults of Melanesia, which to our eyes seem to demonstrate extreme cupidity. The first such cult arose in 1893 when a native prophet in New Guinea announced the coming of a new age of abundance. Gardens would produce yams to overflowing, the trees would bend under their heavy load of fruit, and the dead ancestors would return to inaugurate a new era of plenty. Since then many similar cults have appeared throughout Melanesia. All predict the imminent destruction of the whites there, the return of the dead, and the arrival of a cargo of trade goods (thus the name "cargo cults" for such movements). These cults reached their height after World War II—when the cargo *did* mysteriously appear, usually as drift from torpedoed Japanese and Allied ships or as shot-down aircraft. The cults continue to this day. Recently, for example, the islanders of New Hanover cast their votes in local elections for President Lyndon Johnson. When they were informed that President Johnson was not on the ballot there, the islanders collected money to buy him— because they were convinced that he possessed the secret of obtaining cargo.

All cargo cults believe that outsiders know some secret, of which the natives are deprived, for obtaining the wonderful possessions they have seen outsiders own. The missionaries played a major role in the spread of this belief because they doled out large amounts of trade goods as rewards for conversion. The natives saw the total society of whites and understood unconsciously that religion played an important role—and if they wanted to obtain the riches, beyond imagination, of the outsiders, the simplest thing would be to adopt the religion. But as the natives lined up to be converted, the gifts available for distribution to each convert became proportionately less. Finally, after almost everyone in a local area was converted, the flow dried up altogether. The natives, of course, felt they had been cheated. They no longer received the material benefits of conversion—and they still had not been told the secret of obtaining cargo. In 1933 a missionary in New Guinea reported that he had been told (as translated from pidgin English) by a native spokesman: "How is it we cannot obtain the origin of wealth? You hide this secret from us. What is ours is only rubbish, you keep the truth for yourselves. . . . The white men hide from us the secret of the Cargo."

It was perfectly understandable that the natives should think a secret was involved —for it appeared to them that the cargo arrived as the result of some white ceremonial. The natives had no conception of the manufacturing and distribution processes that lay behind the sudden arrival of ships and airplanes, which unloaded their cargoes at local wharves and airports. The only possible explanation for the natives was that the cargo was the gift of a deity. And why must it be a gift? Because the natives clearly saw that the whites did no "work." Instead they shuffled mysterious papers in offices and obtained their shares of the cargo just by presenting chits at stores. Finally, it must have looked like a ritual of thanksgiving when the whites celebrated the arrival of a ship or airplane: all the whites gathered at the local club, poured each other cocktails, and gossiped with the crews of the ships and airplanes.

So the cargo cults sought to undo the conspiracy, to unlock the mystery. The natives had converted to the Christian religion, but that still did not bring them the secret. So they tried imitating white behavior. One of their number might play the part of a district commissioner sitting in his office closely studying official papers (which, of course, he could not read). The natives lined up on dress parade in the manner of the white police on plantations; they obtained bits and pieces of European machinery, which they tried to use in the ways they had seen whites use them. Recently, in the New Guinea highlands, where people still cultivate their gardens with neolithic tools, the natives erected "wireless towers" like the white man's so that they could communicate with the supernaturals who send the coveted cargo.

The cargo cults clearly support the deprivation theory—but they give an oversimplified view of the kind of deprivation involved in millenarian movements. Not all deprivation experiences are concerned with material goods alone. A person can also be deprived of his status, his own sense of worth, and his traditional patterns of behavior. The experiences of the Navaho Indians of Arizona and New Mexico in the 1930's demonstrate several kinds of deprivation. In previous decades the Navahos had built up herds of sheep and goats, but the herds grew so large that they were overgrazing the land and causing erosion. As a result, the United States government forced the Navahos to kill great numbers of sheep to reduce the livestock to a level that the land could support. In the loss of their sheep many Navahos suffered also a loss of status, for the owner of a large herd could be generous to his many helpers. Now he was little better off than the others. Deprivation occurred, too, because most Navahos felt that something had gone wrong, and people were no longer behaving in the traditional way: for example, Navahos with reduced herds were not as generous as formerly. Still another kind of deprivation they suffered was in their sense of worth. As their contact with whites increased, the Navahos began to feel inferior because, for instance, they ate such "bad" food as prairie dogs.

Many Navahos reacted by becoming members of the Peyote cult. There has been considerable misunderstanding about this cult, which has now been incorporated as the Native American Church of North America. Peyote is a small cactus that grows in southern Texas and the northern half of Mexico. When the flesh or the root of this plant is eaten, it produces physical effects due to its morphine- and strychnine-like constituents, and in most users it produces visions. Many white people believe that the prime appeal of peyote is the pleasurable experiences it supplies, or its addictive quality. But there is no bliss in the taking of peyote (in fact anthropologists report that the taste is bitter and nauseating and the anxiety and depression overwhelming.) It has no comparison with the relief from care provided by opiates or by alcohol. Nor is it addictive. The taking of peyote is strictly a ritualized religious act, in which the individual experiences direct communication with supernatural forces. Like other millenarian cults, Peyote, which is now the main religion among at least fifty major groups of Indians, preaches a moral code of peace and harmony. But it provides special gifts that compensate for the Indians' lack of economic well-being and status. The white man has the Bible and learning—but through peyote the Indian has direct access to God and to revelation. Peyotism makes the Indian the equal of the white, and sometimes his superior, in finding ways to obtain rewards. That is probably the primary appeal of peyote among the Navahos. It enables the user to foresee the plans of the United States government and also to seek new wealth through supernatural help.

A question naturally arises in any examination of millenarian movements: why do they take a religious form instead of simple military or political resistance? The explanation is that religion provides almost the only way for a leader to unite the members of a society. ("Religion" is used loosely to include any exterior, supernatural, and usually mystic force—such as "la grandeur" of Charles de Gaulle or the

Aryanism of Hitler.) By appealing to some superhuman agency, the prophet can avoid identification with any particular group within the society, thus avoiding jealousies and bickering.

One explanation for the rapid spread of the Ghost Dance is that its prophet, Wovoka, was never identified as a member of any particular Indian group, not even his own Paiute of Nevada. By keeping his preaching on the supernatural plane, he demonstrated that his authority transcended that of the local spirits and gods associated with particular lineages, villages, or even whole tribes. Sectional discord was further avoided by the prophet's message to put aside the loyalties of the past, to love one another, and to practice a new moral code.

The most compelling analysis of the stages involved in a millenarian movement—one that applies virtually without exception to those throughout history and around the world—has been made by Anthony F. C. Wallace, Professor of Anthropology at the University of Pennsylvania. He finds that the movements "always originate in situations of social and cultural stress and are, in fact, an effort on the part of the stress-laden to construct systems of dogma, myth, and ritual which . . . will serve as guides to efficient action." He outlines the stages as follows.

1) *The Steady State.* Changes and developments in the culture proceed logically and in sequence; the culture can handle new events. There always exist, of course, some disorganization and stress, but they remain at limits tolerable to most members of the culture.

2) *Period of Increased Individual Stress.* The cultural system begins to lose its equilibrium because of climate change, epidemics, war, conquest by a foreign power, or some other disturbance. As a result, increasingly large numbers of people suffer intolerable stress because it seems to them that their established system can no longer meet their needs. Disillusionment becomes widespread, crime and asocial behavior increase.

3) *Period of Cultural Distortion.* Alcoholism, dishonesty by public officials,

---

> A sense of deprivation
> gives birth to
> the cult. Its driving force:
> religious fervor.
> Its end: the destruction
> of the cult or
> the evolution of a new
> social order.

---

breaches of sexual and kinship customs, gambling, and the search for scapegoats become widespread as people try either to escape from or to circumvent "the system" and "the Establishment." Special-interest groups may resort to violence to compel others to do their bidding. None of these steps, though, is sufficient to restore the equilibrium, and in fact they precipitate the decline in the culture by greatly increasing the stress.

4) *Period of Revitalization.* Once the third stage has occurred, it is very difficult for the culture to return to a steady state without passing through a millenarian movement. Indeed, if such a movement fails to take place, the culture is apt to disintegrate into warring factions or to be absorbed by another, more stable culture. Any successful movement that arises inevitably goes through the following steps:

a) *Formulation of a Code.* A prophet proposes a blueprint for an ideal society that contrasts sharply with the present, disintegrating society. But to convert the existing culture into an ideal one, the faithful must perform a series of duties. Often the mere formulation of the code relieves the stress in the prophet's own personality, and he appears to his followers to be a person miraculously reborn (most of the American Indian prophets, for example, suffered from strange sicknesses or acute alcoholism, from both of which they were liberated almost immediately).

b) *Communication.* The code is now preached to win converts. Those who refuse to accept the code are warned that they have put themselves in material and spiritual jeopardy.

c) *Organization.* The code attracts many converts who differentiate into the few disciples and the masses of followers. The disciples become the administrative organization for the code; they also protect the prophet and combat heresy. The prophet himself usually makes no claim to be a supernatural being—but his followers hold him up as one on whom a supernatural agency has bestowed superior authority that demands unquestioned belief and obedience (witness in this century alone Hitler, Lenin, Mao, Castro, Che Guevara, Father Divine, Elijah Muhammad, and many others).

d) *Adaptation.* The revolutionary movement is in danger because it clearly threatens those interested in maintaining the *status quo.* The disciples adapt by modifying the code and by political maneuver (as did Saint Paul), or they use force if necessary (as did the "holy war" followers of Mohammed). Anyone who deviates from the code is suspect—and is considered a "traitor" if he is a member of the group and "the enemy" if he is an outsider.

e) *Cultural Transformation.* The successful millenarian movement has now won the loyalty of the masses; it no longer is an innovative force in its own society. If the movement worked primarily through religious channels, it establishes a church that preserves the code and maintains, through ritual, public sympathy toward the values that brought forth the new culture. If the movement worked through political channels, it establishes authority through the police, the military, and a bureaucracy.

5) *The New Steady State.* The final step is to bring all aspects of the culture into focus with the basic change made by the millenarian movement. For example, following the success of the Protestant Reformation, a whole series of economic, social, political, and technological changes took place in Europe. The final step is to rewrite the record of the movement and enshrine it in myth and ritual (the Old and New Testaments, the Koran, the collected works of Marx and Engels, and so on). Then a new steady state has been reached.

Clearly, the early Christian church followed this sequence stage by stage, and so did the Protestant Reformation, Mohammedanism, the Handsome Lake religion of the Iroquois, the Third Reich, Mao Tsetung's "cultural revolution," and the Russian Revolution. Even though the Soviets were officially atheistic, they went through all the stages of a successful millenarian movement. In 1917 the entire Russian society was under stress and disintegrating. A prophet, Lenin, arose who miraculously returned from exile across enemy, German territory. He said that he had been in communication with a supernatural being, Karl Marx, who had given him an elaborate code complete with exegesis by another disciple, Engels. An ideal society was preached, and a group of disciples gathered around Lenin (among them Stalin, Molotov, and Trotsky). Mass purges and the execution of tens of thousands of "traitors" enabled the revolutionary movement to adapt, and eventually the entire culture was transformed. The new rulers established their own bureaucracy and secret police to perpetuate the new *status quo*. For all its revolutionary talk, the Soviet Union exists today at a new steady state that forbids the rise of new prophets, such as Mao, or Tito of Yugoslavia, whom it calls a "revisionist."

Very few of the millenarian movements that have occurred around the globe have survived beyond the fourth step of stage four: adaptation. Usually the movement is suppressed by people within its own ranks, as happened to many of the Jewish movements against the Romans, or it is crushed by the military intervention of the established powers (such as the United States sending cavalry to end the Ghost Dance, or the execution of black prophets in Africa by colonial powers). The Melanesian cargo cults have all been doomed to failure for the simple reason that no "secret" was being kept from them; however, out of this ferment new political movements have recently emerged in Melanesia. These movements are attempting to correct deprivation more realistically, and they seem to be succeeding.

Most of the millenarian movements in black Africa have been ruthlessly sup-

The Soviet Union has gone through the five-stage pattern of millenarian movements and reached a new steady state.

pressed by whites, but one that did succeed was the Mau Mau movement of the Kikuyu in Kenya (who based their code largely on the Old Testament). So far the Peyote cult has spread widely and has won the sympathy of professional anthropologists; but it barely escapes repressive measures by its own people and by the state and federal governments, and its prospects for transforming Indian society are not very promising. It appeared several years ago that the Chinese revolution against the Kuomintang was a successfully concluded millenarian movement, but now we know that is not so. Mao's "cultural revolution" shows that it is still only at the cultural-transformation stage and that the victory against external and internal enemies must now be routinized among the Chinese people themselves by getting them to accept a new bureaucracy.

The United States today is plainly in the third stage, the period of cultural distortion. Statistics show that alcoholism has become a major problem and drug use is now widespread. The fabric of sexual mores has broken down, and the younger generation expresses its rebellion against family obligations. A scapegoat is usually found in "the system" or "the Establishment," and all the New Left organizations, particularly powerful on college campuses, have as their aim its destruction. Both the right and the left attack the central bureaucracy, the one accusing it of doing too much and the other of not doing enough. Every month statistics show a steady increase in crime, particularly in crowded urban areas, and people flee the decaying cities to shirk the responsibility of bringing about change. What was a few years ago the alienated behavior of individuals has now become institutionalized in the hippie cult, black militant

groups, and armed rightist organizations. If history and anthropology can tell us anything, it is that the patterns of millenarian movements show that at this point something must happen in the United States, and that it will happen quickly.

But the United States does offer an alternative to millenarian fervor. We possess legal mechanisms that have not yet broken down as did those of the Weimar Republic with the advent of Hitler; they can relieve the stress our culture is now undergoing. Wisdom can now channel the deprivation that so obviously exists at all levels into greater participation by all in the economic and social systems. But should the laws cease to function, the United States will be ripe for a millennial cult. Exactly what form the cult will take cannot now be predicted, for no prophet has arisen whose code appears able to win the support of the masses of the people. It might take the form of a religious movement, as was the rise of Christianity against the Romans, or of a political movement, as was the Russian revolution against the czarists. No matter the form it takes, once begun it is irreversible and almost assuredly will result in violent upheaval. Should no successful millenarian cult emerge to win the loyalty of the masses, then the prospect as taught us by history and anthropology is one of disintegration of our entire society and its eventual disappearance as a viable force, as for example occurred to the Ottomans. Of all the possibilities, plainly one is to be preferred by almost everybody: make the American Dream come true for all by using the legal mechanisms that still exist in our society.

Peter Farb is the author of the widely acclaimed Man's Rise to Civilization As Shown by the Indians of North America from Primeval Times to the Coming of the Industrial State, *which was a selection of the Book-of-the-Month Club for last autumn.*

SMITHSONIAN INSTITUTION, BUREAU OF AMERICAN ETHNOLOGY

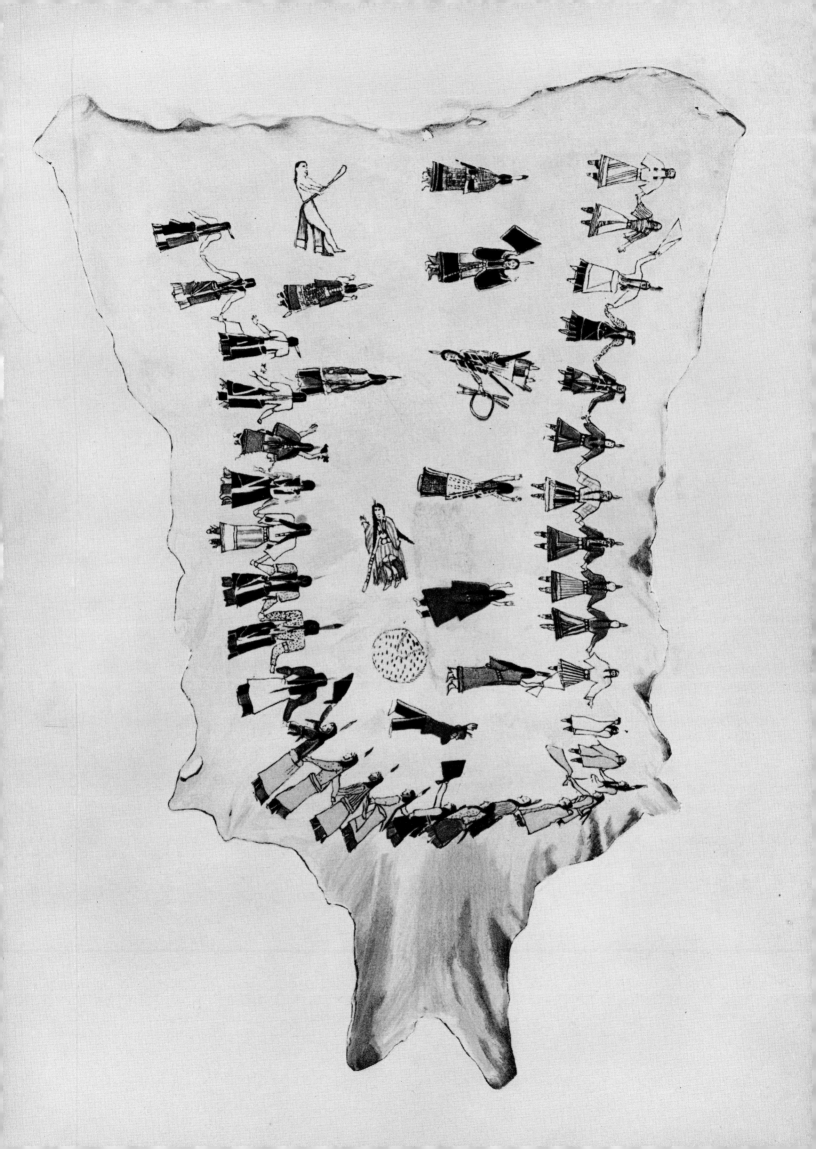

1848

A rebel worker of 1848, above, leads a Paris mob in a detail from Daumier's The Uprising. *Opposite, a 1968 student rebel hurls a paving stone at a Paris police van.*

Again?

A student throws a paving stone. A continent trembles, a world awakes. A student revolt extends to the working class—and its effects reach beyond France, beyond the Continent, as far away as Mexico. It is the spring of 1968, but for many there were haunting reminders of another year of revolution, 1848. And when the reaction of last June caught up with the revolt of May, one's mind recoiled this time to the *triste* end of 1848, when the springtime hopes of an entire continent collapsed in the reaction of counterrevolution. Will 1968, like 1848, be called, in Toyn-

By JOSEPH BARRY

The Men of Order

On the eve of revolt chief advocates of established authority included Prince Metternich, right, foreign minister of the Austrian Empire and architect of the grand conservative alliance forged at the Congress of Vienna. French premier Guizot, opposite, like his king, Louis Philippe, was adamantly against extension of the vote to the bulk of French citizens.

Metternich

The Congress of Vienna, 1814–1815

bee's phrase, a turning point where history failed to turn? Or, as the Germans viewed the earlier revolt, that "crazy and holy year"?

Falling midway between the French Revolution of 1789 and the Russian Revolution of 1917, the uprisings of 1848 had both prophetic and nostalgic elements. The French insurrectionists, wrote Alexis de Tocqueville, who watched them, "were engaged in acting the French Revolution, rather than continuing it." Yet, as Karl Marx predicted, the revolution of 1848 was a rehearsal for a proletarian revolt that would not fail. Did 1968 prepare us for a similar, if yet remote, outcome? The students at the Sorbonne last spring acted out the Paris Commune of 1871, as the students at Columbia played Castro and Che. But will that prove to be the whole story? For 1848 we have near-perfect hindsight; for 1968 we have only a few months of perspective. We are still in the high— or low—tide of its events: not only the French uprisings of last May and the world-wide student unrest are fresh in memory, but so, too, is the harsh suppression by Russia of freedom in Czechoslovakia.

Does reaction follow revolt as inevitably as one tide the other? Or was it simply the swiftness of reaction that was so extraordinary in 1848? In any case, everything about that year has a breathless quality. The Age of Metternich, which had extended from the Congress of Vienna in 1815 ad

infinitum, it seemed, came to a sudden end in February, 1848; and within the next six weeks a dozen conservative rulers fell like so much ripe, if not rotten, fruit.

Yet on the eve of their downfall events seemed under control. Prince von Metternich, the Austrian foreign minister, dominated the Holy Alliance of Russia, Prussia, and Austria, as the Holy Alliance dominated Europe. "Liberalism" and "change" were the upsetting words in Metternich's age: his ideal was an autocratic absolutism tempered by salon wit and supported by a loyal army and police, a submissive bureaucracy, and a grateful church. Ideas of freedom were a sickness to be cured, if in an acute stage of contagion, by bleeding—and the Austrian army was Europe's medical corps, ready and prompt with its treatment. True, France had been feverish with revolt in July, 1830, but in that crisis the *grande bourgeoisie* had merely replaced an anachronistic Bourbon king with the perfect bourgeois monarch: the modest, pear-faced Louis Philippe, Duc d'Orléans.

"'France is bored,'" the political correspondent of *Le Monde* wrote less than two months before the student revolt in May, 1968. He was quoting, with an uncanny parallel, a statement of the poet-politician Alphonse de Lamartine on the eve of the 1848 revolt.

But there was more than boredom that soon shook the French regime of 1848. The revolution of 1789, Lamar-

tine had also pointed out, had simply replaced the "domination of a king by that of wealth . . . instead of one tyrant, there were now several thousand." It was the propertied who constituted *le pays légal*, the legal country: less than 250,000 were privileged to vote in a land of thirty-five million.

As production increased, "society" became richer, but as competition increased, the workers became poorer: wages were lowered as profits went to buy machines. Children as young as six years old stood in front of machines up to sixteen hours a day. Strikes were illegal, unions a criminal conspiracy; but in Paris in February, 1848, hundreds of workers were members of secret societies and clubs.

Paris was still the home of political exiles. The Enlightenment, the Revolution, Saint-Simon ("the golden age of the human race is not behind us, but ahead of us"), Louis Blanc ("equality will not exist until each man . . . produces according to his capacity and consumes according to his needs"), Proudhon ("What is slavery? . . . It is murder. . . . What is property? . . . It is theft"), and, briefly, Marx and Friedrich Engels had made Paris a city of socialist lights.

Republicanism and romanticism, democracy and the industrial revolution, were at work in France. Elsewhere, the fires of revolt were stirred by the spirit of nationalism and self-determination. For decades Italian

François Guizot

King Louis Philippe caricatured as a pear, 1832

leaders of the *Risorgimento* had been agitating for a united, democratic Italy instead of a dozen states and duchies, one third of them directly under the Habsburgs. Similarly, in the thirty-eight states and princedoms of the Germanic Confederation a unifying nationalist spirit was steadily growing, particularly among the students and the more aspiring members of the middle class. In the Austrian Empire the same force created an opposite reaction, as that uneasy conglomeration of subject minorities threatened to fly apart. With the cunning of a Machiavellian prince, Metternich played one force against the other—class against class, nationality against nationality. He garrisoned Austria with Czech regiments and Poland with Austrian regiments, Italy with Hungarian troops and Croatia with Italian.

Troubles, for Metternich, began with street riots in Milan on January 2, 1848. These were followed on January 12 by a more serious revolt in Palermo, Sicily, against King Ferdinand. But the revolutions of 1848 really began in Paris, with a banquet that never took place.

For six months Louis Philippe's more or less loyal opposition had been holding a series of great banquets at which the main entertainment was criticism of his prime minister, François Guizot. The opposition consisted of a handful of deputies, mostly constitutional monarchists, but some, such as Lamartine, republicans; the bulk of it

was the *petite bourgeoisie* clamoring for inclusion in the *pays légal*. Criticism of Guizot's government was again the announced entertainment for the affair of February 22—but this time the government banned the banquet.

Summoned to demonstrate at the Place de la Madeleine by radical newspapers and by club leaders, the people of Paris turned out on February 22, banquet or no. From nine to eleven that morning they stood in the intermittent rain. There were a few cries, a few slogans, some rough humor. Then, at eleven, a great column of students arrived from the Left Bank singing the Marseillaise, their ranks swelled on the way by young workers and artisans. The crowd at the Madeleine became a multitude. It pressed on to the Place de la Concorde and across the Seine to the Chamber of Deputies. Finally persuaded to leave by a company of the National Guard, it returned to the Place de la Concorde. Then, trotting from the Quai d'Orsay, came a platoon of horse troops. The rain was heavy now, and as darkness fell, barricades went up. There was some firing—the first in Paris for a long time—and two women were killed.

The next day King Louis Philippe thought it preferable to call for the National Guard rather than the army. But the National Guard was composed of citizens paying for their own uniforms and fed up with the government, and of officers who wanted the

vote Guizot refused them. In a dozen places that morning, the Guard came *between* the demonstrating crowds and the charging horse troops, and it, too, cried, *"Vive la Réforme!"*

That evening of February 23, along the Boulevard des Capucines, came a cheerful enough crowd carrying torches and flags but no arms. They were stopped by a cordon of troops. A sergeant, writes the French historian Henri Guillemin, "believing the life —or the mustache—of his colonel menaced [by a brandished torch], instinctively pulled the trigger of his rifle." Hundreds of other soldiers fired, and fifty-two demonstrators were dead. The crowd fled one way, the soldiers another. But revolutionaries—or simply angry men—returned, seized a passing tumbrel, piled it with the dead, and solemnly paraded through Paris by torchlight. Now barricades, some with red flags raised above them, sprang up everywhere, across broad boulevards and narrow working-class streets. During the night, with the workers' secret societies and clubs, under *their* leaders, forming hard, organized cores, a riot became a revolution. And at noon the next day Louis Philippe abdicated in favor of his nine-year-old grandson, packed his bags, and fled to London as Mr. Smith.

The grandchild of Louis Philippe was rejected that afternoon in the Chamber of Deputies. The people of Paris had taken possession. Names for

Republicans and Liberals

Most French rebels sought to found a republic, a goal missed in the 1830 revolution. These included Ledru-Rollin, member of the new government, and the poet Lamartine, its guiding spirit. Indirectly allied with the republicans, intellectuals such as the historian Michelet, the poet Hugo, and the novelist Sue drew attention to the need for reform.

Alexandre Ledru-Rollin

The 1830 revolt as seen by Delacroix

the provisional government of the Second French Republic were shouted and noted and finally accepted by the acclamation of the throng. Eighty-one-year-old Dupont de l'Eure was chosen as nominal head of the government and Lamartine as foreign minister, but actual chief, and five other moderates were elected to posts. Through massed, cheering streets the new leaders then marched in a body to the Hôtel de Ville, the town hall of Paris, where revolutionary governments are traditionally proclaimed. There the socialist Louis Blanc and three other radicals were added as secretaries of the government.

There was now a government, including both moderates and radicals, but there was no program. Revolutions rarely come into power with five-year plans. On February 25, thanks to Blanc, the Right to Work was proclaimed in an effort to achieve full employment. On February 26 National Workshops were established for the unemployed, who were an acute problem; they were entrusted, not to Blanc, but to Alexandre Marie, a right-wing minister. Meanwhile Paris was a fete. Amid the celebrants a bishop and a Rothschild danced around newly planted "Trees of Liberty"; bourgeois embraced worker in the name of a bright future.

News of the revolution in France spread like a fever in the Germanies. ("When Paris sneezes," said Metternich, "Europe catches cold.") A student, Carl Schurz recalls, came to

his attic room. Together they "tore down the stairs," raced to the market place, and found it already crowded with young men. "There was no shouting, no noise, only agitated conversation. What did we want there? This probably no one knew; but since the French had driven away Louis Philippe and proclaimed the Republic, something, of course, must happen here too. Some of the students had brought their rapiers, as if it were necessary at once to make an attack or to defend themselves."

Demands from a public assembly in Mannheim brought immediate reforms. In Copenhagen the Danish king met a procession literally halfway with a decree for a new, democratic constitution in his hand. In Munich the king of Bavaria was made to abdicate in favor of his son, a "constitutionalist." Demonstrations caused liberal ministries to be formed in Württemberg, Saxony, and other, smaller states. But above all, there was the astonishing revolt at the heart of the Holy Alliance itself—in the city of Vienna.

The students of Vienna had drawn up a modest petition to Emperor Ferdinand asking for freedom of teaching and study and civic liberties. On March 13, joined by workers and other citizens, they gathered in the streets to present their demands. The speech of a handsome Hungarian patriot named Lajos Kossuth, delivered at the Diet of Pressburg on March 3,

was read to the students, causing great excitement. Before the day was over, soldiers had fired shots into the crowd, and factories in the suburbs were in flames. And on March 13, *mirabile dictu*, Metternich was dismissed and fled, like Louis Philippe, to London. Emperor Ferdinand was forced to promise his people a constitutional government.

In Berlin, the capital of Prussia, Frederick William IV, who saw himself as the father of his people but was in fact a paternal despot, was surprised on March 18 by the sight of barricades. After hours of fierce fighting soldiers had shot down demonstrators during the day, and more barricades had gone up. The king issued a proclamation, pleading to "My Dear Berliners" to remove the barricades, pledging "my royal word" that the streets would thereupon be cleared of soldiers. The soldiers were withdrawn, then the barricades removed, and Prussia was promised a parliament that was to become part of a united Germany.

With Prussia preoccupied and Metternich dismissed, the Holy Alliance—except for holy Russia—was in unholy disorder. Within hours of Metternich's flight Kossuth received the constitution he had demanded, and the Hungarians were close to freedom. The people of Milan rose and, more miraculously, drove out the Austrian army. (It withdrew to fortresses in the east and waited.) The Venetians, too, liberated their city from its Austrian

Alphonse de Lamartine

Jules Michelet

Victor Hugo

Eugène Sue

garrison, and they re-established the Republic of St. Mark. On the same day Charles Albert, king of Sardinia, who many rebels hoped would be the leader of a unified Italy, declared war on Austria.

In France, however, the momentum of February had become the inertia of March. Decrees were not a program. The National Workshops, instead of being models of co-operative productivity, were demonstrations in absurdity—and so their director, Marie, intended. A hundred thousand workers in Paris were marshaled, like a dangerously idle army, for such projects as digging holes in the Champ de Mars and then refilling them. Under pressure and playing for time, Lamartine announced elections by direct manhood suffrage.

Each faction maneuvered for position in the forthcoming elections, which were postponed until late April as a concession to the left. Paris had spoken; the provinces were now to be heard from. Georges Sand, a self-styled "extreme Republican," had few illusions. "Eighteen years of falsehood," she commented, "oppose obstacles to the system of truth, which human breath cannot dispel." (Seven of the nine million who could vote were illiterate.) Meanwhile factories closed, unemployment rose. Workers marched to the Hôtel de Ville. But the countermarches of a new, reorganized National Guard were more impressive—"the personification of so-

ciety defended and refound," in the view of Lamartine. By now his break with the socialists was almost complete. "The elections," he told a friend, "will go against them." In the country "they" were called "communists"—"a name," said Proudhon, "contrived to stir the passions."

Lamartine's middle-class moderates won some five hundred seats in the Assembly; the royalists divided three hundred between the Orléanists, who wanted to restore Louis Philippe or his descendants (two hundred), and the Legitimists, who supported a Bourbon restoration (one hundred). Louis Blanc and his socialist followers polled approximately the same number as the Legitimists.

The formation of a new government was entrusted to the republican Lamartine. But Tocqueville noted, without discontent, that the new Assembly meeting on May 4, in which he was a deputy, contained more great landowners than any under Louis Philippe; the "reds" had been crushed "by the weight of their own dogma—the sovereignty of the people." The balance of power had moved to the right—the right of the propertied.

Elsewhere, April held greater promise. A parliament for all Germany was being elected by direct suffrage to meet in May in Frankfurt, and scarcely a German prince dared oppose it. In Hungary Kossuth initiated reform with wonderful energy, pleasing the Magyars but not the sub-

ordinate Croats and Walachians. In Italy the progress was military—for the most part. After delays the army of Sardinia joined the Milan rebels in a drive against the Austrians. Pressed by the Romans to join the fight against Austria, Pope Pius IX hesitated, sent troops, and then recalled them. He did not want to risk a schism fighting Catholic Austria, he said, and declared the church neutral. Furious, the Romans turned their anger for the Austrians against the pope. From Naples King Ferdinand too had reluctantly sent troops to help the Sardinians and the Milanese, but he withdrew them. He needed them back home. Barricades had been thrown up two days before in his dispute with parliament. Nevertheless the Sardinian army defeated the Austrians at Goito on May 30, and the goal of a free, if not yet united, Italy did not seem far away.

In Paris, matters were moving to a climax. On May 15 a demonstration was called by the club leaders in support of a "free Poland." The Poles, then stirring in rebellion against Russian and German control, were popular in Paris, and defending freedom beyond France was part of the revolutionary tradition. The demonstrators, twenty thousand in number, reached the bridge crossing from the Place de la Concorde to the Chamber of Deputies. Here they found a few troops with a general in charge. "*Vive la Pologne!*" he cried, waving a Polish

The Socialist Camp

Socialists among the rebels followed the late Count Saint-Simon in emphasizing the evil of poverty. Marx was first to see factory workers as a new class, while Blanqui organized the Paris poor. Louis Blanc advocated the right to work, which was made law by the rebel government.

FROM *Album des célébrites industrielles*, PARIS, 1865; LEFT: ARCHIVES PHOTOGRAPHIQUES

Saint-Simon

Steam-driven French soap factory, 1850

flag. He told them they could not cross, then left the center of the bridge open. Was it a provocative invitation to disaster? The crowd swept across the Seine into the Chamber of Deputies. There a radical named Armand Barbès called for war in defense of Poland and a billion-franc tax on the rich; he then led a march to the Hôtel de Ville—followed by no more than five hundred.

At the Hôtel de Ville Barbès proclaimed a new revolutionary government, as well as war against Russia. At this point a National Guard officer burst into the room where Barbès was at work.

"*Who* are *you?*" the officer demanded.

"Member of the Provisional Government," Barbès replied.

"Yesterday's or today's?"

"Today's."

"Then you are under arrest."

More arrests were made. By nightfall the left was decapitated and Lamartine discredited. Was it, then, a provoked coup and a prepared countercoup? "Everything," says a respectable witness, Maxime du Camp, "seems to have been carefully prearranged."

Suddenly, as May drew to a close, the profile of Prince Louis Napoleon Bonaparte, "the Nephew," appeared on countless medallions and matchboxes, in throwaway newspapers and pamphlets, probably financed by French bankers. Twice—in 1836 and 1840—Napoleon's nephew had con-

spired to have himself declared emperor of France, and twice he had failed. The first time he was exiled by Louis Philippe to New York but made his way back. The second time he was sentenced to life imprisonment but escaped to London. Now, just turned forty, Louis Napoleon Bonaparte presented himself as a "working-class candidate" for a seat in the Assembly, and in partial elections on June 4 he was elected by four separate constituencies! As the Chamber debated seating him, he shrewdly resigned, declaring that he reserved himself for whatever duties "the people choose to impose on me."

On June 21 the order went out to close the National Workshops, and two days later the dismissed workers met near the Panthéon and walked to the Place de la Bastille, chanting "Bread or death." Slowly the barricades went up. With them rose not "a certain number of conspirators," Tocqueville testifies, "but one whole section of the population," an entire class of workers "trying to escape their condition. . . ."

The new Minister of War, Cavaignac, now took charge. Strangely, he made no attempt to storm the barricades before they were established. He had other plans: to create a crisis forcing the government to resign and turn power over to him. Fatalistically the workers waited behind their barricades; but during the night they cast bullets, and on Saturday they used them. That morning, convinced noth-

ing else would save them, the deputies gave Cavaignac the full powers he wanted. Carefully he now directed attacks; he was in no hurry. The morale of his troops was good; even the ladies of western Paris came to entertain them.

The attacks reached full savagery on Sunday. By now the barricades in some streets were the height of three men, and the men and women behind them fought with the bravery of the hopeless. On Monday evening, June 26, Tocqueville went to the Hôtel de Ville to get "the day's results." As he walked along the Seine, he met National Guardsmen carrying their wounded. "I observed in talking to them," he writes, "with what terrible rapidity, even in so civilized a century as our own, the most peaceful minds enter, as it were, into the spirit of civil war, and how quick they are, in these unhappy times, to acquire a taste for violence and a contempt for human life. . . ." But his own bloodthirstiness surprised him.

An estimated three thousand "insurrectionists" were killed—many after it was over. They were flung into the Seine, shot or hanged in the streets, in the cemeteries, in their cellar-prisons as they asked for water or bread. From Moscow the czar sent congratulations to Cavaignac for having saved France from communism.

How fared revolt elsewhere? ("in a rebellion, as in a novel," wrote Tocqueville, "the most difficult part to invent is the end.")

The young Karl Marx

Auguste Blanqui

Louis Blanc

In Bohemia the Czechs had won their autonomy, and on June 2 a Pan-Slav congress was held in Prague. But on June 17 Prague was reoccupied by the Austrian General Windischgrätz (to whom the "liberal" Frankfurt parliament sent its congratulations). In Italy the Austrians defeated the Sardinian army in July and reoccupied Milan in August. In October the Russians occupied Bucharest; in November Windischgrätz reoccupied Vienna.

But it was in France, where it had all begun, that December marked the end. A decree that had limited the workday to ten hours now authorized twelve, except where the "nature of the industry" required more. Workers from the closed workshops had been convoyed far from Paris, leaving their families behind to forage in the streets. On November 4 a new constitution, modeled on America's, had been passed by the Assembly. Like America's, it provided for a president elected by universal manhood suffrage. Tocqueville had helped write it; Lamartine's eloquence had ensured its passage. On December 10, elections were held. Nearly seven and a half million Frenchmen voted. These were the results: Lamartine—17,910; Cavaignac—1,448,107; and Prince Louis Napoleon Bonaparte (representing the "Party of Order")—5,434,226.

Postscript, 1849: The Frankfurt parliament finally finished drawing up its constitution and promptly fell apart. In Rome as 1848 ended, the pope was put to flight. He called for help; Louis

Napoleon responded. French troops took Rome and gave it back to the pope. The next month the Austrians recaptured Venice. The Hungarians proved the most stubborn. Austria called on the czar, who gladly obliged; by the end of September, 1849, the Russian commander could write to his czar, "Hungary lies at the feet of your Imperial Majesty."

In two years Metternich returned to Vienna, not at all convinced that his principles had been proved wrong. Nor, in a sense, had they been. If 1848 was the year of the turning point where history failed to turn, it is at least partly because the forces he played, one against the other, played against themselves in their struggles for independence. Instead of Metternich's idea of nationality against nationality, it had become nationalism against nationalism: Slavs against Magyars, Germans against Slavs, with no sense that freedom for all was being lost. Within Germany and Italy, too, rivalries for the domination of a united nation were still as strong as the forces for that unity. And we who have witnessed in 1968 the secessionist movements within nations, from Canada to Nigeria, should be least surprised by the endless Sisyphean labor of making one nation out of a dozen little kingdoms, as revealed in 1848. But the spirit of nationalism had been born and would not be ready to die with the first failures.

As for the rise and quick fall of

libertarian movements, they were to await, like nationalism, a riper moment. In France there was also the prophetic element of a purely proletarian movement. Marx explained its failures: "The bourgeois republic triumphed. On its side stood the aristocracy of finance, the industrial bourgeoisie, the middle class, the petty bourgeois, the army, the *lumpenproletariat* organized as the Mobile Guard, the intellectual lights, the clergy and the rural population. On the side of the Paris proletariat stood none but itself."

In any handbook on How to Steal a Revolution, the first principle, based on the 1848 experience, might well be: insist on immediate, democratic elections. It was a lesson de Gaulle heeded last June when he called for a swift vote to end the risings of 1968. Civil strife, the sound of violence, the great uncertainties, bring cries for the maintenance of order—that is, generally, the old, familiar order. And there is nothing so frightening for a majority as the first stages of a revolution.

On the walls of the student-occupied Sorbonne last May was scrawled: "Universal suffrage is counterrevolution—Proudhon." Lenin and Castro were not to make that mistake.

From his apartment on the rue Jacob in Paris, Joseph Barry watched the spirit of the 1848 revolution revived in the May, 1968, riots. He is presently writing a book about Versailles.

February 23: mob at the rue des Capucines

Protest Becomes Revolution

At the Tuileries on February 21, 1848, Louis Philippe pondered news of angry street crowds and laughed: "It's a storm in a teapot." On February 24 he was fleeing to England. The tumultuous events of the intervening days can be chronicled by the hour and the street. Early on February 23 protestors in Paris were shouting "*A bas Guizot*"—down with the premier. At 2:30 P.M. the king asked Guizot to resign. In the evening a jubilant throng marched to the rue des Capucines to demand that the Ministry of Foreign Affairs light up its offices to celebrate Guizot's fall. The ministry's military guard grew panicky. A fusillade of musket fire raked the crowd, killing fifty-two. As the detail (above) from a contemporary lithograph of the scene shows, there were men in the stricken crowd who did not mistake their opportunity. Radicals raced through Paris, spreading word of the massacre. By the morning of February 24 a hundred thousand Parisians were on the streets building barricades. Overnight the protest had become a revolution. The more daring took the offensive. At the square of the Palais Royale, as depicted in the painting at left, crowds set fire to the Château d'Eau, a military post, and fought with the troops. Bloodied now, the rebels marched on the Tuileries itself. Before they reached the gates, the king had fled, and the French monarchy was no more.

February 24: rebels burn the Château d'Eau

The Frankfurt Assembly

Richard Wagner

The Revolt Spreads: Germany

An ill-kempt worker, opposite, defiantly sitting in the Chamber of Deputies, summed up for one cynical French illustrator the foolish pretensions of the 1848 rebels. Foolish or not, mere news of the Paris revolt stirred an unprecedented spirit of insurgency in the backward principalities of Germany. In Berlin, in mid-March, the bulky autocrat of Prussia, Frederick William IV (below, right), was stunned when his pacific Berliners took to the barricades. "It can't be," he exclaimed. "My people love me." On March 31 in Frankfurt, a hastily formed parliament called for an all-German constitutional assembly to be chosen in the first popular election ever held on German soil. On May 18, 330 elected dignitaries gathered in Frankfurt's St. Paul's Church (above) to draw up a new, liberal constitution for an as yet non-existent German empire. Although it was deliberating in a vacuum—the German princes were not amused—the Assembly raised German hopes high. In Dresden, capital of the kingdom of Saxony, suspicion that the king would not accept the Frankfurt Assembly's constitution spurred the citizenry to attack the city's arsenal and set up a barricade in the nearby street (right). For the help he gave to the insurgents, the conductor of the royal orchestra in Dresden, Richard Wagner, found himself wanted by police. The portrait (above, right) is from the warrant for his arrest.

A Dresden barricade

King Frederick William IV

Lajos Kossuth

The Armed Students
of Vienna

In Vienna, capital of Habsburg despotism, the revolt began with a humble petition to Emperor Ferdinand. Drawn up by students of the Vienna University, it asked the emperor to allow academic freedom and to abolish press censorship. The next day, March 13, the excited students received a copy of a speech delivered earlier at Pressburg by the redoubtable Hungarian patriot Lajos Kossuth. In it Kossuth had boldly announced a truly inflammatory demand—a written constitution for Austria. The students grew exhilarated; on the streets they formed what looked like a threatening mob, and imperial grenadiers shot a few dead. The same day Prince Metternich announced his retirement after forty years in office. Panicked, the advisors of the half-witted emperor decided to give in to all demands, including the students' call for arms. The revolt was on. Overnight the university formed an independent militia, the "Academic Legion," and quickly won over the workers. When the imperial court fled Vienna, the students formed what was virtually a provisional regime. At the great hall of the university, they vetoed government moves, aired grievances, and settled labor disputes. When the government tried to disarm them in May, the students called on their staunchest allies (right), the workers on the Vienna-Gloggnitz railway, and the government had to back down. The students spent their summer vacation of 1848 as rulers of the capital.

Student-led revolt of rail workers

Count Radetsky von Radetz

Giuseppe Mazzini

The Rebel-Patriots of Milan

In Italy revolution broke out on March 18 in Milan, capital of Lombardy. Here established authority was the Austrian Empire, which ruled Lombardy and supported despotic regimes throughout the Italian peninsula. For the Milanese the personal antagonist was Field Marshall Count Radetsky (above), eighty-one-year-old commmander of the imperial army and an enemy of Italian nationalism. It was this vivifying nationalism, above all, that brought all classes of Milan society into the fray, titled aristocrats as well as republican followers of Mazzini (above, right), who rushed from Paris to Milan as soon as he heard news of the outbreak.

On the fateful day itself fifteen thousand Milanese patriots stormed and ransacked city hall. At once, women and children began hauling stones to the rooftops, while the men dug up guns secreted in aristocrats' gardens. Fantastic-looking barricades (at left) made their appearance, heaped high with fine coaches, furniture, and pianos donated by upper-class supporters. A stunned Count Radetsky pulled his troops out of the city and soon after withdrew from the field. In five glorious days the mighty Habsburgs had been routed. When Mazzini's disciple Garibaldi (right) returned to Milan from Uruguay, the new provisional government made the guerrilla leader a general in the revolutionary army.

Giuseppe Garibaldi

Barricade, Borgo della Fontana, Milan

The New Men of Order

Conservative forces soon enough had their day. In France a combination of ballots and bullets put an end to revolt. In June a newly elected middle-class government massacred working-class mobs, leaving the dead at their barricades (opposite). In December Bonaparte's nephew, Louis Napoleon (right), was elected president of the republic and three years later made himself dictator.

In Austria and northern Italy imperial troops regained control, recapturing Milan in August and Vienna in November, 1848. The next month Ferdinand abdicated in favor of his nephew, Franz Josef, shown below being introduced to officials by his prime minister, Prince Felix von Schwartzenberg, who began erasing any trace of revolt. In Rome the uprising against papal rule was crushed in 1849 when Pius IX asked France for aid. In Germany the Frankfurt Assembly's constitution was ignored, and the Assembly passed into history as a might-have-been, like the 1848 revolt itself.

Pope Pius IX

Louis Napoleon as emperor

Emperor Franz Josef

Paris: aftermath of suppression

Frédéric Chopin

CHOPIN
WITHOUT TEARS

He was no sadhearted romantic. His life,
marred though it was by illness,
is plainly a success story—brilliant and brief,
like his masterpieces for the piano

Periodically, the musical world re-shuffles its enthusiasms like a French cabinet in the days of the Fourth Republic. Vivaldi comes, Schumann goes, and Ravel is temporarily banished to a subprefecture in the post-impressionist department. Only Fréd-éric Chopin has been consistently exempt from the general downgrading of romantics that has followed this century's call for clearer music and stronger wine, for Chopin goes on being indispensable to nearly every-body: to the Scarlatti-Mozart-Chopin-Bartók bloc of the Apollonian party as much as to the Beethoven-Berlioz-Chopin-Liszt-Debussy slate of the Dionysians. The acid test of his unique position is that one can still spend three hours at an all-Chopin recital (whether with one's wife or one's favorite girl) without feeling hope-lessly trapped for the evening. Would one consider going to an all-Liszt, an all-Brahms, or even an all-Beethoven

recital? I doubt it. To be marched up the hill and then down again more than once by any of the other roman-tics exhausts one's capacity for identi-fying with the *Sturm* and the *Drang*. But one can undergo a hundred Chopin climaxes without experiencing the ennui attendant on a single Liszt *Liebestraum.*

If there are ever doubts about him, they are expressed *sotto voce* and rather apologetically; one does not like to disparage Chopin any more than Shelley. The last time anyone could bring himself to do it was in the 1920's, I believe, and then not actually in public but in a private conversation between the composer Bernard van Dieren and Ferruccio Busoni, also a composer and one of the two or three great virtuoso pianists of the century.

Busoni (growing uneasy about the Chopin ballades): . . . What I want to know is whether you see anything in these pieces beyond their surface

charm, their romantic appeal.

Van Dieren: I am afraid I see noth-ing but waltzes.

Busoni: That is exactly what I find myself. All Chopin's music is waltzes, *and* waltzes.

Van Dieren: I don't think that is the worst. But they are always the same waltzes. It must have struck you that Chopin invariably repeats the same expositions. His only idea of form is a further repetition on a large scale of what he has already said twice.

Busoni: That is one of his faults. I try to make the best of his music, yet I cannot bring myself to believe in it. . . .

The upshot was, apparently, that Busoni went on playing Chopin, with results as brilliant as Horowitz's. From all accounts he had a "terrifyingly grandiose conception of Chopin," and he was a Lisztian at heart—that was the root of the trouble. They were both great virtuoso composers, of

By FREDERIC V. GRUNFELD

This is Eugène Delacroix's sketch for a painting of Chopin playing the piano for his mistress, George Sand. The canvas was eventually cut in two by a dealer, to double his profit. At right is the half showing Sand, standing enraptured; on the opposite page is the portrait of Chopin from the other half.

George Sand

course, but where Liszt was an extrovert, a great actor and a man of the experimental theatre, Chopin was inner-directed, a man of the salons whose light shone brightest "in the bosom of the half-tenebrae of a summer night," as one of his friends expressed it. It is almost impossible for a pianist to play both of them equally well. "They play Chopin as if it were Liszt," André Gide once noted. "They do not understand the difference. Thus presented, better Liszt."

What fascinated Gide about Chopin was the element of chance that seems to govern his music; the sense of never knowing where the next chord is going to fall. It sounded to Gide as though Chopin's modulations were forming under his very fingers, like a landscape revealing itself only gradually to the wanderer's eye; the music surges up spontaneously "as if he were improvising; that is, he seemed to be constantly searching for, inventing

and discovering his thoughts little by little. . . . I see no other meaning in the titles he was fond of giving to certain of his most exquisite pieces: *Impromptus.*"

This is what has always intrigued the intellectuals and the literati, whether Heine or Proust or T. S. Eliot or Thomas Mann, though the point is usually missed by the pianists, whose main concern, after all, is to convey a sense of assurance rather than of uncertainty. I have heard Rubinstein, on occasion, play Chopin as though the next turn of phrase were unpremeditated, but few virtuosos have mastered the knack. As his friend Hector Berlioz pointed out, "Scarcely anyone besides Chopin can play this music and give it the character of something unexpected, unforeseen, which is one of its principal charms." We know that the young Liszt, already the greatest pianist of the century, was "magically enthralled" when he heard

this style for the first time, and according to his pupil Moriz Rosenthal, it was Chopin's playing—rather than the experience of hearing Paganini—that sent Liszt back to the piano for four years, practicing six hours a day and "trying to develop his individuality so he could reach Chopin."

Years later, after Chopin's death, Liszt, together with that effusive bluestocking, the Princess Sayn-Wittgenstein, wrote a book about him; and though it is a hopelessly muddled affair in most respects, it does provide us with expert testimony on this one important point: what was it, precisely, that people called "*le secret de Chopin*" and other pianists found impossible to duplicate? It reposed in the "fluctuations," the "wavy, undecided motion" of his playing, Liszt decided. "Through his peculiar style of performance, Chopin imparted this constant rocking with the most enchanting effect; this making the melody

undulate to and fro, like a skiff driven over the tossing waves."

Chopin's manuscripts sometimes carry the words "tempo rubato" ("robbed" or "stolen" time) to indicate that he wanted them to deviate from a strict metrical beat; Liszt says that he expected everything to be played rubato, whether it was marked that way or not. "All of his compositions should be played with this accentuated and measured swaying and balancing. It is difficult for those who have not frequently heard him play to catch the secret of their proper execution." Difficult as it may have been in Liszt's day, it is even more so now, when pianists are expected to conform to the dry-eyed musicological manner: just play the notes please. And yet, far from being merely a stylistic device, these "sonorous effects of a vaporous fluidity of which only he knew the secret" (the pianist Marmontel speaking this time) are somehow central to his whole work, and spell out what he was trying to achieve beyond surface charm. If there is a certain graphology in sounds—"a new sound proclaims the new man who makes it," says Schoenberg in the *Harmonielehre*—then it may also give us some insight into the riddle of the historical Chopin, this curiously misunderstood composer about whom so much has been written, and who said so little about himself. Indeed, his friends assure us that the man and his music were in complete agreement; as the contemporary Bohemian pianist Ignaz Moscheles testified, he even looked like his music. The French playwright Ernest Legouvé has a passage in his *Souvenirs* in which he recalls that the personality of Chopin left him just as strangely affected as his "unknown and mysterious" music.

"I cannot give a better definition of

A carriage stands waiting outside the door of George Sand's house, Nohant, where Chopin spent seven summers. His black top hat strikes a formal note alongside her butterfly net and picnic baskets.

Chopin than to say that he was a *charming trinity*," Legouvé writes. "There was such a harmony between his person, his way of playing the piano, and his works that it seemed as though they could no more be separated than the various features of a face. The particular sound he drew from the piano was like the glance of his eyes; the slightly ailing delicacy of his fingers was allied to the poetic melancholy of his nocturnes, and the careful attention he conferred on sartorial details helped explain the worldly elegance of certain parts of his work. He gave me the impression of being the natural son of Weber and a duchess; the thing I called his three selves formed one."

This famous bon mot about Chopin's paternity is quoted so often because it sums up everything so neatly: Weber, too, was not only a great romantic but also a consumptive who died young. The trouble with the image is that it takes into account only the nocturne Chopin and not the composer of the polonaises. It was easy for his friends to see him as the archetype of the doomed, romantic artist because he was so perfectly cast for the role. They realized that he was "the most sensitive genius in existence" and somehow failed to notice his extraordinary inner strength. But a composer who dies of tuberculosis at thirty-nine and yet produces what Chopin did cannot have been "dying all his life," as Berlioz suggested; he had to possess heroic energy and even a kind of cunning, the hardheaded managerial sense usually attributed to businessmen rather than artists. For despite all the hindrances that man and nature could contrive to place in his path, Chopin created more than two hundred works—not all of them masterpieces, but with a far higher ratio of the imperishable to the ephemeral than is usually the case.

The sorrows of Chopin, so easily turned into a film script, should not obscure the fact that this is essentially a success story, cut along classic lines:

young man of humble origins conquers foreign capitals, hobnobs with celebrities, dines with princes, nor loses common touch. He may have been George Sand's spoiled child, but the core of this man was rockhard and quite unspoilable. Schumann, who knew him only slightly, sensed this in his music and spoke of "cannon buried in flowers."

This is the dualism of *piano* and *forte*, of elegance and power, of free-roaming right hand and strict left hand, of French and Polish, that runs through his entire life. Everyone knows that he was born in Poland—on March 1, 1810, in the village of Zelazowa Wola, twenty-eight miles from Warsaw—but the significance of that fact, like so much else about him, has been seriously disputed. The Poles, naturally enough, see him as their national poet. Others have expressed doubts. "I never can understand why Chopin should be regarded as a Polish composer," writes the critic Cecil Gray. "His father was a Frenchman; he lived the whole of his actively creative life in France and the predominant influence on his work is Italian—the influence chiefly of Bellini." Even so, Chopin's Polishness went deeper than the color of his passport. From a musical standpoint, in fact, it was of paramount importance because of the way Polish folk music shaped his whole thinking on questions of rhythm and melody. His formal training, we know, was based on the standard German repertoire of his day—including, notably, Bach's *Well-Tempered Clavier*. That may seem far removed from the Chopin we know, but playing Bach was a habit that remained with him for the rest of his life. "I stay home for two weeks before each concert, playing nothing but Bach," he confided to a pupil many years later. "That is all my preparation: I don't practice my own things at all."

But if Bach was one cornerstone of the Chopin edifice (and the subtle

Born in the room at left in the Polish village of Zelazowa Wola, Chopin could play his mother's "giraffe" piano by the time he was six. Above is the drawing room at Nohant, where Delacroix, Liszt, and Heinrich Heine were frequent visitors.

counterpoint of many of his pieces confirms it), then another was the Polish peasant music he heard on all sides as he was growing up. It gave him a taste for an entirely different kind of melody than the foursquare German triad-tunes that dominate the symphonies and sonatas of the German romantics. Although the very term "folk music" had not yet been invented—the eastern European aristocracy still referred to it as "coachman's music," because they always heard their coachmen singing it—we know that Chopin was thoroughly familiar with it. Since he used to listen to this music and play it when he went to the country for the holidays, most of his first compositions were mazurkas and polonaises. That he listened to the peasants very carefully is substantiated by one of the boyhood "newspapers" that he sent to his parents in 1824, when he was fourteen, reporting his summer adventures in the third person:

FOREIGN NEWS

29 August 1824. As he was passing through Nieszawa Mr. Pichon [Chopin] heard a village Catalani [a famous soprano] singing at the top of her voice as she sat on a fence. His attention was at once caught and he listened to both song and voice, regretting, however, that in spite of his efforts he could not catch the words. Twice he walked past the fence, but in vain—he could not understand a word. Finally, overcome by curiosity, he fished out of his pocket three *sous* and promised them to the singer if she would repeat her song. For a time she made a fuss, pouted and refused, but, tempted by the three *sous*, she made up her mind and began to sing a little mazurka . . . "See, the wolf is dancing there behind the mountains; He's breaking his heart because he hasn't got a wife."

The curious thing about this item is that it might have been taken almost verbatim from Béla Bartók's travel notes, when he went song hunting in rural Hungary at the beginning of the twentieth century; one of Bartók's letters, in fact, describes a very similar experience in almost identical words. The rhythm of the mazurka, furthermore, performed precisely the same service for Chopin's music as the Hungarian *verbunkos* did for Bartók's; it liberated him from the foursquare "classical" rhythms of the conven-

tional tradition—the ONE-two-three-four of the march, and the SLIDE-two-three of waltz time. Mazurkas are song-based country dances from the plains of Mazowsze (Mazovia), where Warsaw is located; their usual time signature is three-four or three-eight, but Chopin's mazurkas are so irregular in their rhythm that Meyerbeer once insisted, when he heard Chopin play one of them, that it was really in two-four. Another musician, Charles Hallé, caught him playing a mazurka in four-four and proved it by counting out the beats, whereupon Chopin, laughing, explained that this was the national way of doing things. Wanda Landowska, who used to play Chopin on her harpsichord because he sounded so folkish that way, remembered in later years that in the Polish countryside near Kielce, where she grew up, "I saw, as a child, a farm girl milking the cows, in two-four time, while soothing them by singing a mazurka in three-four time. This, which seems incredible to a stranger, is natural for a Pole because of the peculiar accentuation of the mazurka."

Here, at any rate, is one of the rea-

Chopin gave his first public concert, at the age of eight, in the recital hall, below, of the Radziwill Palace in Warsaw. During a rainy winter spent on the island of Majorca, left, he had to play on "a poor instrument rented locally."

sons why Chopin was taken to task by a few Viennese critics in 1829 for his recklessly unrhythmical playing and for what they called "the non-observance of the indication by accent of the commencement of musical phrases." And that, of course, is precisely what Chopin's music sets out to do; instead of coming down with a thump on the obvious downbeat of a phrase, his accents come at unexpected places, so that it seems as though he has allowed his rhythms to get out of hand, just as he has let the harmonies slip through his fingers without bothering to get a firm grip on the tonic. These idiosyncracies did not prevent him from being, at nineteen, the foremost pianist in Warsaw, a local prodigy obviously destined for a larger, better illuminated stage. In 1829 he left Poland, and after eight inhospitable months in Vienna (where, under more favorable circumstances, he might have become the logical successor to Beethoven and Schubert) he made his way to Paris. In Stuttgart, en route, he learned that the Polish rebellion had been crushed by the Russians, and tradition has it that the Revolutionary Etude was

prompted by the appalling news.

But the Paris of 1831 promptly restored his spirits. It was the ideal home for him—a city of brilliant young men bringing romanticism to full flower: Balzac, Victor Hugo, Alfred de Vigny, Sainte-Beuve, Mérimée, the elder Dumas, Alfred de Musset, Théophile Gautier, and Gérard de Nerval. Stendhal, of the older generation, had just published *The Red and the Black*. The Baroness Aurore Dudevant—better known to her readers as George Sand—was working on her first successful novel, *Indiana*. Ingres and Delacroix, the Chopin and Liszt of French painting, were producing some of their best pictures.

Chopin's literary counterpart was the exiled poet Heinrich Heine, also just arrived in Paris—"standing all alone," as Ford Madox Ford describes him; "perhaps the most exquisite of all the world's lyricists since the great Greeks, perhaps the greatest of all the world's realistic-bitter romantics." Like Chopin, Heine was a revolutionary of the spirit who had not gone off to the wars, having found sundry good reasons to "keep me here in

amorous dalliance/ while others fight the Grand Alliance." His notes on Chopin show that it was a case of instant recognition, for as Liszt also testifies, "At a glance, a word, a tone, Chopin and Heine understood each other." Chopin, said Heine, made him forget all about the mechanics of keyboard virtuosity and let him descend into a private abyss, "into the painful loveliness of an art that is as profound as it is delicate."

Soon after arriving in Paris, when the Polish Prince Radziwill had introduced him to Society at the Baron Rothschild's, Chopin was able to charge fifteen or twenty gold francs (an enormous sum in those days) for an hour's lesson. He moved to the modish rue de la Chausée d'Antin, bought a carriage, and patronized the best tailors. "I have my place among ambassadors, princes and ministers without knowing myself how I got there," he wrote to a friend in Warsaw, but it could not have escaped him that his attractiveness to the ladies had something to do with it. "His blue eyes were more spiritual than dreamy," is Liszt's description of him during these years. "His fair hair was soft and silky, his nose slightly aquiline, his bearing so distinguished and his manner stamped with so much high breeding, that involuntarily he was always treated *en prince*."

It was Liszt who introduced him to George Sand in 1836, when she was thirty-two and Chopin twenty-six. Already the most talked-about woman in France, she was the mother of two half-grown children and of a great many books, mainly about the trials and triumphs of women in love. She had weathered stormy liaisons with Alfred de Musset and other men of talent, and now it was Chopin's turn; one has the impression that she decided to make him her lover for his own good. They celebrated their honeymoon in the sight of heaven on the island of Majorca, where they lived for two months in the abandoned monastery of a hillside village. Chopin suffered a severe attack of consumption, which drove them back to France just as his piano finally caught up with them, and from then on they left Paris only to spend the summers at Nohant, Sand's family estate near Châteauroux.

Sand, often cast as the villain of the piece, actually did wonders for him by protecting him from the buffetings of the world. At Nohant, under her careful management, he could escape to another kind of island—a sprawling manor house in the style of Louis XVI, surrounded by woods, fields, and gardens. He played games with the children, improvised at the piano for guests, rode a donkey while others took long walks in the woods, and organized a puppet theatre that can still be seen at Nohant. But at the same time he fretted and agonized over his compositions. Sand writes that "he shut himself up in his room for whole days, weeping, walking, breaking his pens, repeating a bar a hundred times, writing and effacing it as many times, and recommencing the next day with

a minute and desperate perseverance. He could spend six weeks over a single page, only to write it at last as he had noted it down at the very first."

In Paris during the winter months, when Nohant was too cold for them, Chopin could also "toil like the devil over every composition" (as he wrote to a friend), but with fewer results. There were too many distractions. Living with Sand in the rue Pigalle and later on the Square d'Orleans, they were the center of a brilliant literary and artistic circle. Balzac, with his interior decorator's eye, described their Pigalle headquarters to Countess Hanska: "Sand's dining room furniture is of carved oak. The color of her little salon is café au lait and her drawing room is full of superb Chinese vases, filled with flowers. . . . The magnificent piano is upright, square and of rosewood. Chopin is always here. She smokes nothing but cigarettes. She does not get up until four o'clock; at four, Chopin has finished giving his lessons. . . ."

His very infrequent concerts were attended by "the most elegant women, the most fashionable young people, the most famous artists, the richest financiers, the whole elite of society, the aristocracy of birth, fortune and beauty." He still gave piano lessons, mainly to members of this same leisure class, "but there are few who *au fond* understand me." His health was steadily declining; in time he weighed less than a hundred pounds. "I have no time to be sick," he told his pupils. Despite Sand's care, he began to feel edgy and discontented. As their lovers' quarrels grew more frequent and intense, each side had cause to consider itself maltreated. Their final rupture, in August, 1847, had to do with a family row over the marriage of Sand's headstrong daughter. Some of their friends sided with him; others defended her for having borne this "cross" for so long.

"I do not regret that I helped her through the eight most difficult years of her life," he writes afterward, not

very convincingly. "I do not regret what I have suffered." What mattered was that she had imposed a working order on his life; cut adrift, he stopped producing new music. To console himself he went on a seven-month tour of Britain, playing in London and "dragging round the Scottish palaces," but the whole desperate undertaking was merely a protracted preamble to death. He died in Paris, of laryngeal tuberculosis, on October 17, 1849, less than five months short of his fortieth birthday.

During the sixteen prolific years in France prior to the break with Sand, Chopin had produced an uninterrupted stream of masterpieces on such a consistently brilliant level of craftsmanship and invention that it is quite impossible to talk of "early," "middle," and "late" Chopin. They are masterpieces with conspicuously modest titles that are as quietly understated as their message: études, preludes, scherzos, ballades, etc. These were not then established categories of music; it was Chopin who invested them with the meaning they now possess. The impromptus preserve some of the freedom and spontaneity of his legendary improvisations. The nocturnes are his serenades, his "night music." The preludes are descended from the purposeful prefaces that introduce Bach's fugues, but Chopin uses the term to designate poems and mood pieces of the most diverse kinds —"preludes to meditation," as Gide calls them. The waltzes are society music, freely (and undanceably) adapted from the newly fashionable ballroom whirl. The scherzos, related to Beethoven's sonata scherzos, display the "lofty, virile energy" that Chopin could muster at critical mo-

From this window Chopin gazed across the Square d'Orleans in Paris at the lights in George Sand's apartment. It was in this haunting atmosphere that he composed his famous Berceuse, *a draft of which is seen lying on the desk.*

ments. Some of the ballades are said to have been inspired by certain Polish poems, but their meaning is not of the literary world, or susceptible to line-for-line analysis. The études, supposedly designed as exercises for the hand, actually celebrate the triumph of music over technology.

He always liked short, self-contained forms in preference to the established concerto and sonata precedents. Both of his great piano sonatas —the Funeral March in B-flat minor, Opus 35, and the B minor, Opus 58— are open to the charge of lacking a strong unifying line, of breaking down into unrelated compartments. Schumann said of Opus 35 that the composer had simply "yoked together four of his wildest children" to make a sonata, but such structural flaws are hardly serious enough to prevent either work from occupying a central place in the keyboard repertoire.

The Polish pieces, in a class by themselves, brought the folk dance into the concert hall, paving the way for a spate of ruder, more spectacular nationalisms—Mussorgsky's Russian operas, Falla's Spanish ballets and Bartók's Hungarian concertos, among others. For Chopin, accustomed to writing them since boyhood, the polonaises were always an occasion for discharging the cannon concealed beneath the flowers and for demonstrating his ability to play muscular *fortes* as well as a hundred shadings of *piano*. The mazurkas, fifty-six of them, have to do with what Liszt calls "coquetries, vanities, fantasies, inclinations, elegies, vague emotions, passions, conquests, struggles. . . ." Few writers on Chopin have been able to resist the temptation to wax similarly poetic over this music, though no composer illustrates more graphically the truth of Heine's dictum that music begins where words fail. The stock metaphors used to run to "black velvet roses," "solitary cries of despair," "sunny cobwebs in a summer breeze," or "little Polish flowers carried by a strong wind," but they have lately been replaced by the sterner stuff of modern rationalist criticism: "rhapsodic geometry" and "mathematical sublimities," whatever they might be. Chopin himself fought a losing battle to keep his admirers from pinning unauthorized labels to his pieces; it drove him wild when women gushed, "Play me your 'Second Sigh,'" or "I love your 'Bells.'" Faced with the problem of describing a new work to a distant friend, however, he would sometimes venture out on a metaphorical limb of his own. The slow movement of the E-minor Concerto, for example, was supposed to convey "the impression you get when your eye wanders over a moonlit landscape on a cool spring night, a landscape you know well and love much." But the important thing to Chopin was the ultimate musical effect. "Have I made it haunting?" he asks. "I wonder—time will tell."

If he had any real doubts on this point, they must have been dispelled by his reception among the leading *cognoscenti* of his day. Chopin usually met with nothing less than complete and spontaneous approval. Schumann greeted his Opus 2 with the famous cry, "Hats off, gentlemen: a genius!" Felix Mendelssohn told his friends about one of the Chopin preludes: "It is so beautiful that I could go on forever playing it over and over, all the more because by no possibility could I have written it." Posterity has had no reason to revise those judgments. On the contrary, as the art of dissonance has progressed, it has also become clear that Chopin, not Wagner, was the real father of modern chromatic harmony. As Thomas Mann points out in *Doctor Faustus*, there are things in Chopin that anticipate and even surpass Wagner's most revolutionary episodes. "Take the C-sharp minor Nocturne, Opus 27, No. 2, and the duet that begins after the enharmonic change from C-sharp minor to D-flat major," says Mann's twelve-tone composer, Adrian Leverkühn. "That surpasses in despairing beauty of sound

Racked by spasms of coughing, Chopin succumbed to tuberculosis in his apartment at 12 Place Vendôme on the morning of October 17, 1849. The death mask and cast of his right hand were made by a sculptor, August Clesinger, the same day.

all the Tristan orgies—even in the intimate medium of the piano . . ."

Were ours not the noisiest of all possible worlds, Chopin might have been preserved for us, like Purcell, as a monument to some bygone delicacy, and as a poet's composer—"so intimate, this Chopin, that I think his soul/ Should be resurrected only among friends," says T. S. Eliot. But circumstances have transformed him into a colossus of the decibels, a creature of loudspeakers, magnetic tape, and celluloid. Legions of pianists have nearly succeeded in pounding this most private of composers into a mass of public bits. Every aspiring virtuoso regards himself ex officio as a Chopin interpreter, and annual competitions are held to find the fairest of them all. Every now and again one of his pieces is squeezed and tortured into a pop ballad like "I'm Always Chasing Rainbows." Yet even then some of the original incandescence usually breaks through the murkiest arrangement and manages to seduce the public ear. He is no respecter of classes, obviously, this composer who wrote for the snobbiest audience in Europe; for now every level of taste in the hierarchy of music appreciation has its favorite Chopin: the conservatory professor, the Philharmonic Society subscriber, the man with the radio. There is something powerful and indestructible about music that can survive its own popularity this way. It will certainly not disappear until the last piano has come unstrung.

Before writing on behalf of the deromanticalization of Chopin, Frederic V. Grunfeld appealed for the un-anthropologicalization of totem poles (Autumn, 1968) and the re-beatification of the Beatles (in Spring, 1968).

THE LASCAUX PUZZLE

Perhaps we will never know the real meaning of
the paintings in the French cave until one disturbing question
is finally answered: whom were they done *for?*

By ROY McMULLEN

The enchantress Hyperbole and her sister Analogy are well known to admirers of prehistoric cultures and can be credited with some remarkable achievements: our readiness, for instance, to see a Venus in almost any steatopygic pendulous-breasted figure. In no place, however, have their spells been quite so evident as in the study of the French cave of Lascaux.

This most famous of all Upper Paleolithic sites has been called the birthplace of art, the Sistine Chapel of prehistory, the Chartres cathedral of the Stone Age, and the quietus for all our notions of progress. It has been described as a laboratory for making hunting magic, a place for initiating boys into manhood, a shrine for fertility rites, a temple dedicated to metaphysical maleness and femaleness.

Its horses have been compared with those of Apollo and those in T'ang dynasty painting, its deer with those in Scythian metalwork, and its bulls with those of ancient Mesopotamia and Minoan Crete. Its seemingly abstract rectangles, checkerboards, ovals, circles, chevrons, barbs, rods, dots, and dashes have been read as huts, traps, combs, blazons, excrement, wounds, weapons, sexual symbols, and snares for souls.

Above, horses, deer, and four huge bulls, the largest (center) eleven feet long, circle the main hall of Lascaux

PHOTOGRAPHS BY RALPH MORSE, *Life* MAGAZINE © TIME INC.

The "dead man" scene (page 97) has stirred some of the liveliest speculation, partly because it contains the only identifiable representation of a human being in the entire cave and partly because of the figure's beaked head and evident state of sexual excitement. The idea that a hunter has been killed by a bison he has wounded, and that the bird-topped stick is a spear-thrower (many such ornamented weapons have been found at Stone Age sites), has been deemed too simple. More typical of the thinking of today's experts is a theory, based on an assumed parallel with Siberian legends, that the painting represents a fight between two shamans, one of whom has taken the shape of a bison. In this context the bird on the stick is interpreted as a "spirit-helper."

The shaman, defined by Webster as "a priest-doctor who uses magic to cure the sick, to divine the hidden, and to control events," is also a fashionable candidate-by-analogy for the role of the supposedly typical Lascaux artist (and of the supposedly typical Upper Paleolithic artist, for of course the theories concern cave art in general). One of his advantages over other analogous personages—the African Bushman rock-painter, for example—is that he exists, or has until fairly recently, among primitives whose cultural patterns supposedly resemble those of the Ice Age hunters; he has been found among the Eskimo, the Lapps, and several peoples of northern Siberia. Another of his advantages is that he is usually an artist with a special relationship to animals; he is said to talk their language. And still another, I suspect, is that his powers are broad enough and vague enough to permit the construction of some wonderful chains of analogies.

I do feel that we can yield too easily and too often to the spells of Hyperbole and Analogy. We ought to remember how little we really know about Lascaux and concentrate on the few relatively firm facts and strong

probabilities we have. We ought also to remember that the people who created Lascaux were painters, whatever else they may have been. As such they can be partly understood even by atomic age nonshamanists.

And as such they raise, for me at least, a profoundly troubling question—a question oddly neglected by the analogizing experts.

But first some facts and probabilities. Lascaux is a Y-shaped cave near the town of Montignac, in the Dordogne department of southwestern France. It is one of the smaller of the underground Paleolithic sites, the total length of its corridors being only a little more than a hundred yards. Its paintings were almost certainly executed over a period of several generations, perhaps centuries, but the time of greatest activity seems, on the basis of stylistic analysis and carbon-14 dating, to have been about 15,000 B.C.

Although this was during the last ice age in Europe, we should not think of the Lascaux hunters as spending their lives slogging over the frozen tundra. The climate in the Dordogne region may have been about like that of central Canada today, with pleasant summers. The typical Lascaux painter probably lived in a rock shelter with a windscreen of animal skins, in a lean-to, or even in a clay-floored hut; in any event he did not inhabit his decorated cave. He was familiar with grease-burning lamps, needles, and fairly efficient, elegantly ornamented stone tools and weapons. In sum, he was not at all the nasty lowbrow de-

scribed in fiction about the Ice Age.

This last fact leads me to another, the importance of which, for anyone who thinks about pictures, cannot be overstressed. It is this: scientists are now reasonably sure that the biological evolution of Homo sapiens stopped somewhere around forty thousand years ago. In other words, as far as native endowment goes, the typical Lascaux artist (he was many individuals, of course) was just as well off as Robert Rauschenberg or Andrew Wyeth. He had the same clever hands, the same binocular vision, and the same integrating brain. Most significantly for our present meditation, he had the same symbol-making capacity.

Of course he lacked certain modern painting techniques, and he could not make use of the aesthetic sophistication and historical awareness that are available to Rauschenberg and Wyeth. But he had his own methods and his own academic traditions.

Hence to refer to Lascaux as the birthplace of art is to trade a high mystery for a cheap piece of romanticism. Art is forever being born, and its birthplace is the nature of Homo sapiens. We ought to avoid being condescending in our judgment of the achievement of the typical Lascaux artist. One way of being condescending is to be excessively tender toward him: to ignore, for example, the plain truth that his crudely scribbled "dead man," whatever interest it may have for anthropologists, is poor stuff by any artistic criterion. And another, more subtle way of being condescend-

TEXT CONTINUED ON PAGE 105

THE ANIMALS OF LASCAUX—A PORTFOLIO

On the succeeding pages are seen some of the creatures—and the enigmas—that throng the walls of a cave known only since 1940, when four boys followed their dog Robot down a hole opened by an uprooted tree. Opposite is the "dead man," seemingly victim of a wounded bison. Curiously, the depiction of human figures, when they appear at all in Paleolithic art, is crude in comparison to that of animals. The next spreads show in turn: first, a painted and engraved black cow seven feet long and a line of horses (the rear hoofs of the cow rest on multicolored squares that have been variously interpreted as hunting snares or tribal insignia); second, in a gallery off the main hall, a frescolike ceiling decorated with cattle and horses, the latter somewhat reminiscent of those in Chinese art; third, bulls, horses, and deer, seen in a detail from the main hall, which may have been painted and repainted over a period of centuries; and finally, the shaggy little horses on the last page of the portfolio, whose perpetual gallop may be ended by a mysterious green mold that for the past decade has been eating away paintings that have survived thousands of years in solitude and darkness. The cave is now closed.

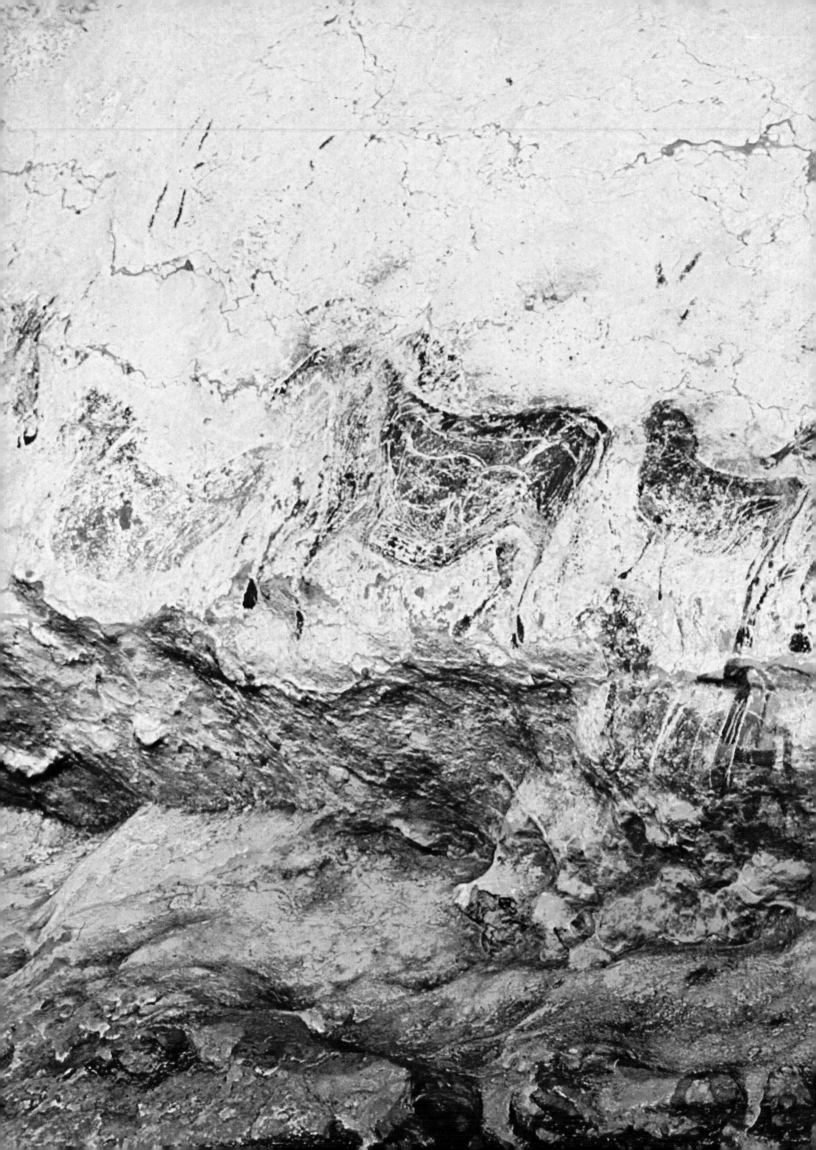

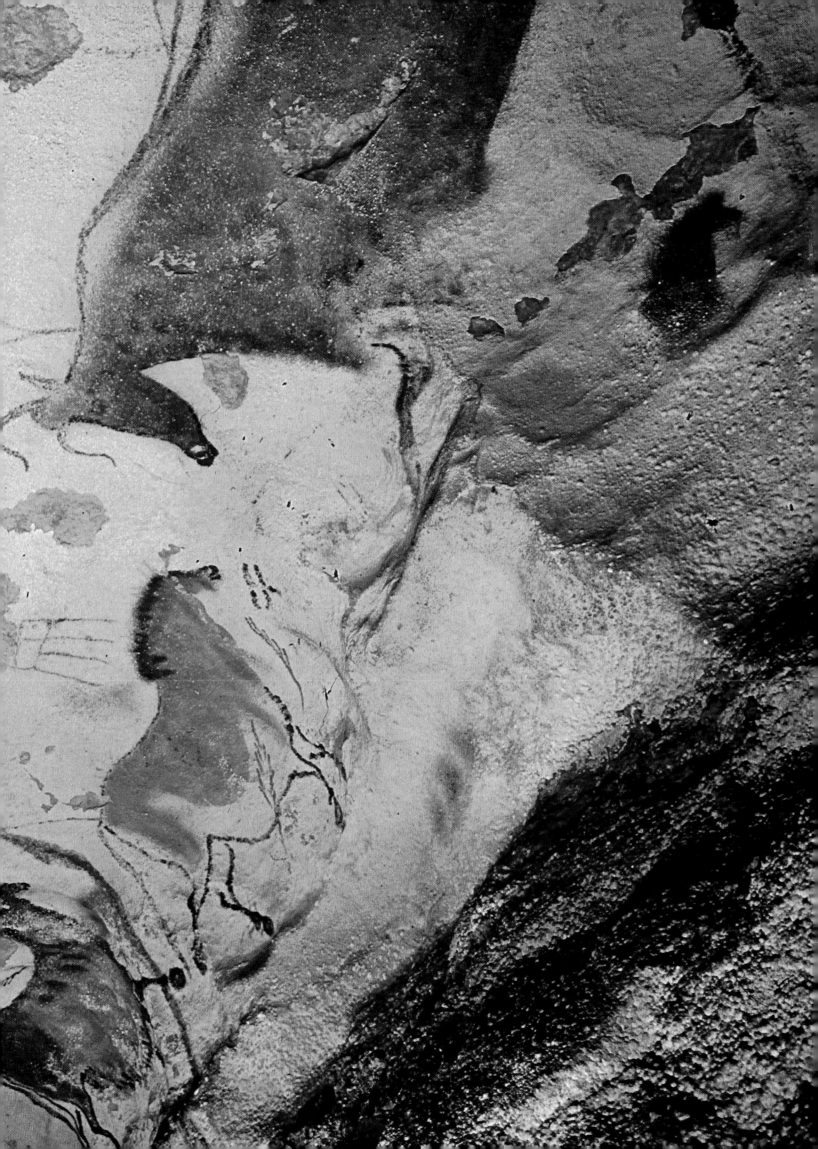